Prion Humour Classics

SAMPLER

PRION

All titles in the *Prion Humour Classics* Sampler
published in 1999 & 2000 by
Prion Books Limited
Imperial Works
Perren Street
London NW5 3ED

email: books@prion.co.uk
Visit our website: **www.prionbooks.com**

The sampler is provided free of charge to booksellers
as a promotion for the *Prion Humour Classics* series

ISBN 1-85375-409-9

Cover image courtesy of The Advertising Archives
Printed and bound in Great Britain
by Creative Print & Design, Wales

Contents

PRION HUMOUR CLASSICS

Augustus Carp Esq	Henry Howarth Bashford
Seven Men and Two Others	Max Beerbohm
Mapp and Lucia	E F Benson
How Steeple Sinderby Wanderers Won the FA Cup	J L Carr
The Diary of a Provincial Lady *	E M Delafield
The Papers of A J Wentworth, BA	H F Ellis
Squire Haggard's Journal	Michael Green
The Diary of a Nobody	George and Weedon Grossmith
Three Men in a Boat	Jerome K Jerome
Mrs Caudle's Curtain Lectures	Douglas Jerrold
Sunshine Sketches of a Little Town	Stephen Leacock
No Mother To Guide Her	Anita Loos
The Autobiography of a Cad	A G Macdonell
The Serial *	Cyra McFadden
The World of S J Perelman *	S J Perelman
The Education of Hyman Kaplan *	Leo Rosten
The Return of Hyman Kaplan *	Leo Rosten
The Unrest-Cure and other beastly tales	Saki
The English Gentleman	Donald Sutherland
My Life and Hard Times *	James Thurber
Cannibalism in the Cars	Mark Twain

* for copyright reasons these titles are not available in the USA or Canada in the Prion edition.

INTRODUCTION

> "A classic is something that everybody wants to have read and nobody wants to read."
>
> Mark Twain

At the risk of sounding like a Marxist (a Groucho Marxist, that is), I'd like to say: humour has never been taken seriously. Yet 'humour', as Robertson Davies said, 'which foolish people value so lightly, is precious stuff.'

All life can be found in comedy – some would argue, more so than with its serious sibling, tragedy. As Howard Jacobson says of one of the 'little books' in our current series: 'it makes you wonder why you ever spent so much time on *War and Peace*.' The lack of epic status means humour books are rarely allowed to join the literary pantheon, yet with minor chords they create their own particular kind of 'everyday' epic. As faint praise they are often tagged with the term 'minor classic'. And of course, by minor classic, people usually mean a classic more readable than the major kind. A classic, against Mr Twain's better judgement, that you really do want to read.

There is something rather guilt-ridden in the attitude that anything which goes down so easily can't be legitimate, immutable art. Humour is invariably thought of as 'literature on holiday': light-hearted works by those usually engaged in, and soon to return to, the more noble pursuits of serious journalism and the novel. Yet for some, humour is the beginning and the end: an art form, a genre, a whole world.

Some of the world's great humorists – Stephen Leacock, S J Perelman, James Thurber among them – were accused of arrested development: an unwillingness to progress to longer, more serious works. But humour should be valued on its own terms. Like judging Picasso on his realism, or barracking Woody Guthrie for never producing a symphony, it is kind of missing the point.

Though he or she works in miniature, the great humorist creates an entire universe with its own logic, and a line of their prose is instantly recognisable. Yet one-liners, jokes and quotes can't convey a flavour of their world. Not until you are fully immersed can you really appreciate it. And once within the grasp of its warped geometry everything becomes funny.

There are many reasons the books featured in the Prion Humour Classics series might have dropped out of print in the past, but never because they have failed to make us laugh. A major cause has been their ability to defy categorisation: many are fictions but not quite novels or traditional stories. Yet they're not really non-fiction either. Writers like Jerome K Jerome, Max Beerbohm, Mark Twain, James Thurber and S J Perelman mix autobiography with fantasy and experimentation in a way few novelists would dare. Their genre-bending playfulness has often been their very downfall.

Some have been forgotten because they are one-book wonders: a nugget of genius in an otherwise undistinguished career. Some, like Mark Twain, remain in print but hidden among the worthy and unappetising classics and are never anthologised with an accent on humour. Some are buried in the fiction section, classed, rather awkwardly, as honorary novels. But many, after initial popularity, are pushed out of the humour section in the bookshop into a literary limbo to make room for next season's cut-and-paste TV tie-ins and topical joke books.

Yet there is such a thing as a humour classic: a neglected but coherent popular art form that originated in the Grub Street periodicals of the early 19th-century and stretches all the way to today's bestselling favourites like Bridget Jones and Adrian Mole. It began in particular with the birth of *Punch* in the 1840s – an era of rough and ready journalism that produced genius on the scale of Dickens and Thackeray. At roughly the same time the newspapers of the American West, in the hands of men like Mark Twain, Ambrose Bierce and Bret Harte, were filling their columns with their own brand of humour. Indeed Twain tapped into the new American vernacular and indigenous sense of humour so successfully that he virtually single-handedly invented modern American literature.

So many of the great works of humour started as journalism. In the days before television, it was the vast array of periodicals and newspapers that provided the man and woman in the street with their fun. These entertainments – sometimes one-off sketches, sometimes serials or regular columns – occasionally produced something simultaneously more universal and zeitgeisty than most celebrated novels of the same period. Ostensibly hack projects spawned works of genius such as Jerome K Jerome's *Three Men in a Boat* and George and Weedon Grossmith's *The Diary of a Nobody*, which both entertained and reassured a nation as it made fun of the pretensions of the new Victorian middle-classes.

And it wasn't just men at work in these lower reaches of journalism. Woman writers, from the likes of Mrs Gaskell, Mrs Oliphant and Mary Ann Evans onward, have often found the jobbing world of magazines a more sympathetic outlet for their writing than the rarefied gentleman's arena of the novel. Our series features books from such diverse talents as Anita Loos and E M Delafield, both of whom wrote successful humorous works in the 1920s and 30s that started off as serials in women's magazines before gaining the wider recognition they deserved between hardcovers.

If *Punch* was the magazine most responsible for making the English laugh at themselves for over a century, *The New Yorker* magazine became the modern American bastion of humour. Founded in 1925 by Harold Ross, it went on to nurture the Algonquin set and is responsible in part for almost every great American humorist of the last century: Dorothy Parker, Robert Benchley, James Thurber, S J Perelman, A J Liebling, Ludwig Bemelmans and Woody Allen. In contrast to Twain's muscular vernacular, *The New Yorker* writers were post-Freudian sophisticates with an urbane and neurotic line in humour that helped fellow Americans laugh at the insanities and inanities of modern life.

At last with Prion Humour Classics, an on-going library, classic humour has found a permanent home. The series has cornered the best books in the field in a single swoop and features the works of every notable humour author. Several of the titles are brand-new selections geared for a modern readership. Each is reintroduced by a famous present-day author – from Woody Allen to Will Self and Kathy Lette to Jilly Cooper. Each is a careful act of literary restoration, many having the original artwork and illustrations reinstated – stylish-looking hardbacks at paperback prices.

One of the great pleasures of reading these books, which range between 20 and 150 years old, is the shock of just how sharp they still sound to our modern ear. It seems that the best jokes have been around longer than you'd think: Mark Twain – the orginal stand-up comedian – has had several of his sketches adopted wholesale by the Monty Python team; comic scenes straight from Dickens have been re-assembled on the Fast Show; without Thurber and Perelman we'd have no Woody Allen or Jerry Seinfeld; without Stephen Leacock no Garrison Keillor; without Anita Loos no Helen Fielding. *Three Men in a Boat* – Vic Reeves' favourite book – is simply Men Behaving Badly in 19th-century London; Mr Pooter is every inch the Victorian Victor Meldrew; the world of *Augustus Carp Esq* is as black as anything The League of Gentlemen have dreamt up; Mrs Caudle was nagging her poor husband a hundred years before Vera Duckworth or Mildred Roper took up the cudgels; while Michael Green's Squire Haggard set a template for Blackadder when Richard Curtis and Rowan Atkinson were still undergraduates at Oxford.

Make no mistake, though, our series is not an act of gentle reverence – celebrating a bunch of doddery old humorists who've managed to keep faintly in touch with the young guns of today. These oldies are more than capable of outstripping almost anything in contemporary humour. You know the imitations, now try the originals.

Andrew Goodfellow, Prion
July, 2000

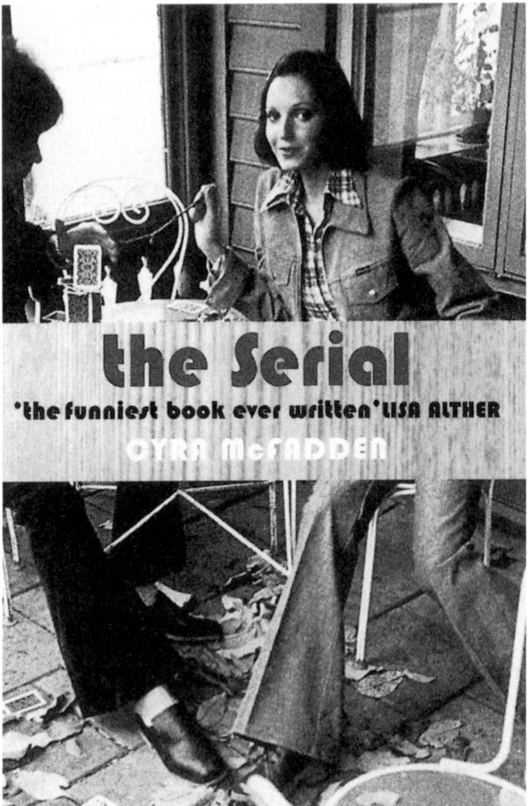
the Serial
'the funniest book ever written' LISA ALTHER
CYRA McFADDEN

The Serial

A YEAR IN THE LIFE OF MARIN COUNTY

CYRA McFADDEN

with a new preface by the author

"the funniest book ever written"

Lisa Alther

The Serial is an adult soap opera of Californian hippie excess. Kate and Harvey Holroyd are desperate to stay part of the fast set in the hip and happening Marin County of the 1970s, where the free spirit ideals of the late '60s have become commodified and trend-obsessed. Natural fibres and organic produce are de rigueur and everyone talks in the psychobabble of faddish self-help manuals whilst spending their time rebirthing themselves, zen jogging or visiting the pet psychiatrists. The soap follows the paths of Harvey and Kate as they attempt to keep up with their way-out neighbours, little realising that, along with everyone else in Marin, their lives are a hilarious parody of the straight world from which they have tried to escape. Illustrated with the original pictures by Tom Cervenak.

April 2000
1-85375-383-1
£8.99

Hip wedding on Mount Tam

As she got ready for Martha's wedding, Kate reflected happily that one great thing about living in Marin was that your friends were always growing and changing. She couldn't remember, for example, how many times Martha had been married before.

She wondered if she ought to call her friend Carol and ask what to wear. Martha had said "dress down," but that could mean anything from Marie Antoinette milkmaid from The Electric Poppy to bias-cut denims from Moody Blues. Kate didn't have any bias-cut denims, because she'd been waiting to see how long they'd stay in, but she could borrow her adolescent daughter's. They wore the same clothes all the time.

Her husband, Harvey, was already in the shower, so Kate decided on her Renaissance Faire costume. She always felt mildly ridiculous in it, but it wasn't so bad without the conical hat and it was definitely Mount Tam wedding. Now the problem was Harvey, who absolutely refused to go to Mount Tam weddings in the French jeans Kate had bought him for his birthday. She knew he'd wear his Pierre Cardin suit, which was fine two years ago but which was now establishment; and when he came out of the shower, her fears were confirmed.

Since they were already late, though, there was no point in trying to do something about Harvey. They drove up Panoramic to the mountain meadow trying to remember what Martha's bridegroom's name was this time (Harvey thought it was Bill again, but Kate was reasonably sure it wasn't) and made it to the ceremony just as the recorder player, a bare-chested young man perched faunlike on a rock above the assembled guests, began to improvise variations on the latest Pink Floyd.

Right away, Kate spotted Carol and knew her Renaissance dress was all right—marginal, but all right. Carol was wearing Marie Antoinette milkmaid, but with her usual infallible chic, had embellished it with her trademark jewelry: an authentic squash-blossom necklace, three free-form rings bought from a creative artisan at the Mill Valley Art Festival on her right hand, and her old high school charm bracelet updated with the addition of a tiny silver coke spoon.

Reverend Spike Thurston, minister of the Radical Unitarian Church in Terra Linda and active in the Marin Sexual Freedom League, was presiding. Kate was thrilled as the ceremony began and Thurston raised a solemn, liturgical hand; she really got off on weddings.

"Fellow beings," Thurston began, smiling, "I'm not here today as a minister but as a member of the community. Not just the community of souls gathered here, not just the community of Mill Valley, but the larger human community which is the cosmos.

"I'm not going to solemnize this marriage in the usual sense of the word. I'm not going to pronounce it as existing from this day forward. Because nobody can do that except Martha and"—he held a quick, worried conference with somebody behind him—"and Bill."

Harvey was already restless. "Do we have to go to a reception after this thing?" he asked too loudly.

"Organic," Kate whispered, digging her fingernails into his wrist. "At Davood's."

Harvey looked dismayed.

"These children have decided to recite their own vows," Thurston continued. Kate thought "children" was overdoing it a little; Martha was at least forty, although everybody knew chronological age didn't matter these days. "They're not going to recite something after me, because this is a *real* wedding—the wedding of two separatenesses, two solitarinesses, under the sky."

Thurston pointed out the sky and paused while a jet thundered across it. Kate thought he looked incredibly handsome with his head thrown back and his purple Marvin Gaye T-shirt emblazoned with "Let's Get It On" stretched tightly across his chest.

"Martha," he said, "will you tell us what's in your heart?"

Standing on tiptoe, Kate could just catch a glimpse of the bride; slightly to the right of her, she spotted Martha's ex-husband-once-removed with his spacy new old lady, who, Kate thought, looked like Martha. She tried to remember which of Martha's children, all present and looking oddly androgynous in velvet Lord Fauntleroy suits, were also his.

Martha recited a passage on marriage "from the Spanish poet Federico García Lorca." Last time she was married, she'd said "Frederico." Kate thought the fact that Martha had got it right this time was a good sign; and she adored the Lorca.

When Bill recited in turn, he was almost inaudible, but Kate thought she recognized *The Prophet*, which was not a good sign. She dug her fingernails into Harvey again; he was shifting his feet restlessly. This wasn't a sign of anything, necessarily, since Harvey simply couldn't get used to his new Roots, but it was best to be safe.

"Hey, listen," she whispered to Carol, who had wiggled

her way through the crowd and was now at her side. "It's terrific, isn't it?"

"Really," Carol whispered back. "He looks good. He's an architect that does mini-parks. She met him at her creative divorce group."

Kate leaned across her to take in the crowd. She thought she recognized Mimi Fariña. She also noticed Larry, her shampoo person from Rape of the Locks, who always ran her through the soul handshake when she came in for a cut and blow-dry. She hoped she wouldn't have to shake hands with Larry at the reception, since she never got the scissors/paper/rock maneuvers of the soul handshake just right and since she was pretty sure that Larry kept changing it on her, probably out of repressed racial animosity.

Thurston, after a few remarks about the ecology, had just pronounced Martha and her new husband man and woman. Kate felt warmly sentimental as the bride and bridegroom kissed passionately, and loosened her grip on Harvey's wrist. She noticed that the fog was beginning to lift slightly and gazed off into the distance.

"Hey, look," she said to Harvey excitedly. "Isn't that the ocean?"

"The Pacific," Harvey replied tersely. "Believed to be the largest on the West Coast. It's part of the cosmos."

Kate felt put down. Harvey was becoming increasingly uptight these days, and remarks like this one were more frequent. Look at the way he'd baited her TA instructor at the Brennans' the other night. "You are not O.K.," he had told him loudly, lurching slightly in his Roots. "I could give you a lot of reasons; but take my word for it—you are *not* O.K."

Yes, Kate was going to have to do something about Harvey....

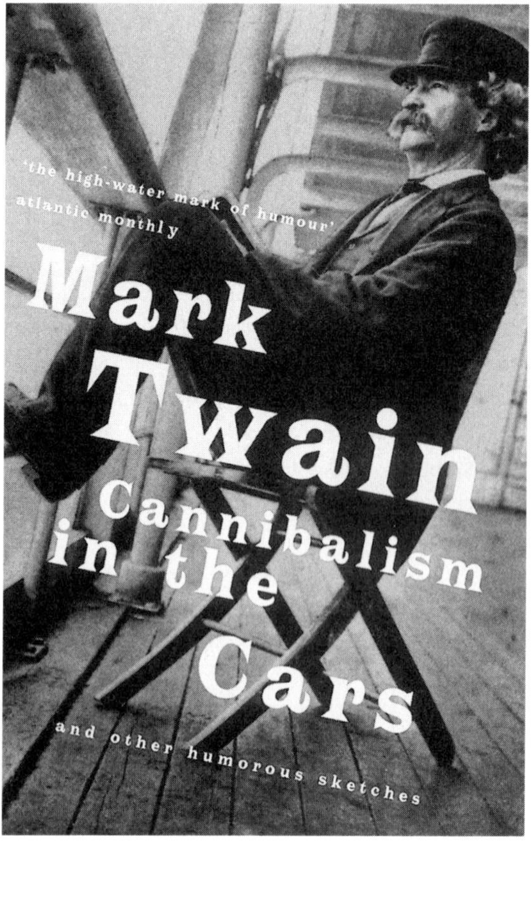
'the high-water mark of humour'
atlantic monthly
Mark
Twain
Cannibalism
in the
Cars
and other humorous sketches

CANNIBALISM IN THE CARS

THE BEST OF TWAIN'S HUMOROUS SKETCHES

MARK TWAIN

with a new introduction by ROY BLOUNT JR

"the high-water mark of humour"

Atlantic Monthly

Cannibalism in the Cars is a selection of the funniest sketches from the rambunctious father of all cynics. Twain's sardonic sketches on everything from politicians, tourists, preachers, journalists, barbers, nagging wives, devious children and gullible low-lifes are as hilarious and universal today as they were when Twain hammered them out to make a name for himself in the 1860s.

In these freewheeling exuberant tales, Twain's mischievous love of pranks, hoaxes, tall tales, slapstick and parody is shown to best effect as he weaves violence, cruelty and the plum stupidity of human nature into comic gold, making us roar with laughter at our own idiotic self-deception and vain conceit.

April 2000
1-85375-369-6
£8.99

Running For Governor

A FEW months ago I was nominated for Governor of the great State of New York, to run against Mr. John T. Smith and Mr. Blank J. Blank on an independent ticket. I somehow felt that I had one prominent advantage over these gentlemen, and that was—good character. It was easy to see by the newspapers that if ever they had known what it was to bear a good name, that time had gone by. It was plain that in these latter years they had become familiar with all manner of shameful crimes. But at the very moment that I was exalting my advantage and joying in it in secret, there was a muddy undercurrent of discomfort "riling" the deeps of my happiness, and that was—the having to hear my name bandied about in familiar connection with those of such people. I grew more and more disturbed. Finally I wrote my grandmother about it. Her answer came quick and sharp. She said—

> "You have never done one single thing in all your life to be ashamed of—not one. Look at the newspapers—look at them and comprehend what sort of characters Messrs. Smith and Blank are, and then see if you are willing to lower yourself to their level and enter a public canvass with them."

It was my very thought! I did not sleep a single moment that night. But after all I could not recede. I was fully committed, and must go on with the fight. As I was looking listlessly over the papers at breakfast I came across this paragraph, and I may truly say I never was so confounded before.

"PERJURY.—Perhaps, now that Mr. Mark Twain is before the people as a candidate for Governor, he will condescend to explain how he came to be convicted of perjury by thirty-four witnesses in Wakawak, Cochin China, in 1863, the intent of which perjury being to rob a poor native widow and her helpless family of a meagre plantain-patch, their only stay and support in their bereavement and desolation. Mr. Twain owes it to himself, as well as to the great people whose suffrages he asks, to clear this matter up. Will he do it?"

I thought I should burst with amazement! Such a cruel, heartless charge. I never had *seen* Cochin China! I never had *heard* of Wakawak! I didn't know a plantain-patch from a kangaroo! I did not know what to do. I was crazed and helpless. I let the day slip away without doing anything at all. The next morning the same paper had this—nothing more:—

"SIGNIFICANT.—Mr. Twain, it will be observed, is suggestively silent about the Cochin China perjury."

[*Mem.*—During the rest of the campaign this paper never referred to me in any other way than as "the infamous perjurer Twain."]

Next came the *Gazette*, with this:—

"WANTED TO KNOW.—Will the new candidate for Governor deign to explain to certain of his fellow-citizens (who are suffering to vote for him!) the little circumstance of his cabin-mates in Montana losing small valuables from time to time, until at last, these things having been invariably found on Mr. Twain's person or in his 'trunk' (newspaper he rolled his traps in), they felt compelled to give him a friendly admonition for his own good, and so tarred and feathered him, and rode him on a rail, and then advised him to leave a permanent vacuum in the place he usually occupied in the camp. Will he do this?"

Could anything be more deliberately malicious than that? For I never was in Montana in my life.

[After this, this journal customarily spoke of me as "Twain, the Montana Thief."]

I got to picking up papers apprehensively—much as one would lift a desired blanket which he had some idea might have a rattlesnake under it. One day this met my eye:—

"THE LIE NAILED!—By the sworn affidavits of Michael O'Flanagan, Esq., of the Five Points, and Mr. Snub Rafferty and Mr. Catty Mulligan, of Water Street, it is established that Mr. Mark Twain's vile statement that the lamented grandfather of our noble standard bearer, Blank J. Blank, was hanged for highway robbery, is a brutal and gratuitous LIE, without a shadow of foundation in fact. It is disheartening to virtuous men to see such shameful means resorted to to achieve political success as the attacking of the dead in their graves, and defiling their honored names with slander. When we think of the anguish this miserable falsehood must cause the innocent relatives and friends of the deceased, we are almost driven to incite an outraged and insulted public to summary and unlawful vengeance upon the traducer. But no! let us leave him to the agony of a lacerated conscience (though if passion should get the better of the public, and in its blind fury they should do the traducer bodily injury, it is but too obvious that no jury could convict and no court punish the perpetrators of the deed)."

The ingenious closing sentence had the effect of moving me out of bed with despatch that night, and out at the back door also, while the "outraged and insulted public" surged in the front way, breaking furniture and windows in their righteous indignation as they came, and taking off such property as they could carry when they went. And yet I can lay my hand upon the Book and say that I never slandered Mr. Blank's grandfather. More: I had never even heard of him or mentioned him up to that day and date.

[I will state, in passing, that the journal above quoted from always referred to me afterward as "Twain, the Body-Snatcher."]

The next newspaper article that attracted my attention was the following:—

> "A SWEET CANDIDATE.—Mr. Mark Twain, who was to make such a blighting speech at the mass meeting of the Independents last night, didn't come to time! A telegram from his physician stated that he had been knocked down by a runaway team, and his leg broken in two places—sufferer lying in great agony, and so forth and so forth, and a lot more bosh of the same sort. And the Independents tried hard to swallow the wretched subterfuge, and pretend that they did not know what was the *real* reason of the absence of the abandoned creature whom they denominate their standard-bearer. *A certain man was seen to reel into Mr. Twain's hotel last night in a state of beastly intoxication.* It is the imperative duty of the Independents to prove that this besotted brute was not Mark Twain himself. We have them at last! This is a case that admits of no shirking. The voice of the people demands in thunder-tones 'WHO WAS THAT MAN?' "

It was incredible, absolutely incredible, for a moment, that it was really my name that was coupled with this disgraceful suspicion. Three long years had passed over my head since I had tasted ale, beer, wine, or liquor of any kind.

[It shows what effect the times were having on me when I say that I saw myself confidently dubbed "Mr. Delirium Tremens Twain" in the next issue of that journal without a pang—notwithstanding I knew that with monotonous fidelity the paper would go on calling me so to the very end.]

By this time anonymous letters were getting to be an important part of my mail matter. This form was common—

"How about that old woman you kiked of your premisers which was beging. POL PRY."

And this—

"There is things which you have done which is unbeknowens to any-body but me. You better trot out a few dols. to yours truly, or you'll hear thro' the papers from HANDY ANDY."

This is about the idea. I could continue them till the reader was surfeited, if desirable.

Shortly the principal Republican journal "convicted" me of wholesale bribery, and the leading Democratic paper "nailed" an aggravated case of blackmailing to me.

[In this way I acquired two additional names: "Twain the Filthy Corruptionist," and "Twain the Loathsome Embracer."]

By this time there had grown to be such a clamor for an "answer" to all the dreadful charges that were laid to me that the editors and leaders of my party said it would be political ruin for me to remain silent any longer. As if to make their appeal the more imperative, the following appeared in one of the papers the very next day:—

"BEHOLD THE MAN!—The independent candidate still maintains silence. Because he dare not speak. Every accusation against him has been amply proved, and they have been endorsed and re-endorsed by his own eloquent silence, till at this day he stands for ever convicted. Look upon your candidate, Independents! Look upon the Infamous Perjurer! the Montana Thief! the Body-Snatcher! Contemplate your incarnate Delirium Tremens! your Filthy Corruptionist! your

Loathsome Embracer! Gaze upon him—ponder him well—and then say if you can give your honest votes to a creature who has earned this dismal array of titles by his hideous crimes, and dares not open his mouth in denial of any one of them!"

There was no possible way of getting out of it, and so in deep humiliation, I set about preparing to "answer" a mass of baseless charges and mean and wicked falsehoods. But I never finished the task, for the very next morning a paper came out with a new horror, a fresh malignity, and seriously charged me with burning a lunatic asylum with all its inmates, because it obstructed the view from my house. This threw me into a sort of panic. Then came the charge of poisoning my uncle to get his property, with an imperative demand that the grave should be opened. This drove me to the verge of distraction. On top of this I was accused of employing toothless and incompetent old relatives to prepare the food for the foundling hospital when I was warden. I was wavering—wavering. And at last, as a due and fitting climax to the shameless persecution that party rancor had inflicted upon me, nine little toddling children, of all shades of color and degrees of raggedness, were taught to rush on to the platform at a public meeting, and clasp me around the legs and call me PA!

I gave it up. I hauled down my colors and surrendered. I was not equal to the requirements of a Gubernatorial campaign in the State of New York, and so I sent in my withdrawal from the candidacy, and in bitterness of spirit signed it, "Truly yours, *once* a decent man, but now

MARK TWAIN, I. P., M. T., B. S., D. T., F. C., and L. E."

1870

THE WORLD OF
SJ PERELMAN
"The funniest writer in America since—himself"
GORE VIDAL
INTRODUCTION BY WOODY ALLEN

The World of S J Perelman

S J PERELMAN

with a new introduction by WOODY ALLEN

"the funniest writer in America"

Gore Vidal

Entering the warped world of S J Perelman is a unique comic experience. His scalpel-keen satirical sketches lampoon the screaming absurdities of modern life and bring succour to that most persecuted minority of all: the embattled sane. The star of the sketches is Perelman's own mock-sombre and eternally put-upon fictional persona, who merely craves a little peace but is continually pushed closer to the edge by the intrusions and idiocies of others from movie moguls to dry cleaners. The first collection to cover every decade of Perelman's writing, *The World of S J Perelman* is a brand new selection of his finest pieces, many of which have been unavailable for years. To many he is simply the most original and funniest humorist of the twentieth century.

June 2000
1-85375-384-X
£8.99

Portrait of the Artist as a Young Mime

"Song Without End" features the highlights of Franz Liszt's life.... The music was recorded by Jorge Bolet, one of America's foremost pianists.... Most dramatic story behind the scenes of the making of "Song Without End" was the coaching of Dirk Bogarde by Victor Aller to enable the actor to give a flawless visual performance at the keyboard to match Bolet's already recorded score. Mr. Aller, a master pianist, also is Hollywood's best known piano coach for stars. Dirk Bogarde had never played a note in his life! Not only did he have to learn how to play the piano—he had to learn to play like genius Franz Liszt.

—*The Journal-American.*

The day started off, as all mine do, at a snail's pace. I got to my studio on Carmine Street about a quarter of ten, closed the sky-light and lit the kerosene stove—oxygen, however essential to aeronautics and snorkeling, is death to the creative process—and settled down with the coffee and Danish I pick up every morning en route from the subway. Then I emptied the ashtrays into the hall and washed out a few brushes, meanwhile listening to WQXR and studying the canvas I had on the easel. Shortly before eleven, I ran out of excuses for cerebration and began mixing my colors. That's inevitably the moment some nuisance takes it into his head to phone, and in this case it was the bloodiest of them all—Vetlugin, my dealer. His voice trembled with excitement.

"Did he call you? What did he say?" he asked feverishly. Good old Vetlugin, the Tower of Babble. He opens his mouth and out comes confusion; the man has an absolute genius for muddle. By valiant effort, I finally extracted a modicum of sense from his bumbling. Some Hollywood nabob named Harry Hubris, reputedly a top producer at Twentieth Century-Fox, was clamoring to discuss a matter of utmost urgency. Ever quick to sniff out a kopeck, Vetlugin, in direct violation of orders, had promptly spilled my whereabouts. "I figured it'd save time if he came down to see you personally," he cooed. "The precise nature of what he wants he wouldn't reveal, but I smelled there must be dough in it."

"Listen, you Bessarabian Judas," I groaned. "How many times have I told you never, under any circumstances, to divulge—" Like all arguments with leeches, this one was futile; muttering some claptrap about ingratitude, he hung up and left me biting my own tail. It was a half hour before I calmed down sufficiently to resume work, but I knew the jig was up when the doorbell rang, and one look at the character bounding upstairs confirmed my fears. From his perky velvet dicer to the tips of his English brogues, he was as brash a highbinder as ever scurried out of Sardi's. The saffron polo coat draped impresario-fashion over his shoulders must have cost twelve hundred dollars.

"Say, are you kidding?" he exclaimed, fastidiously dusting a bit of plaster from his sleeve. "Those terrific abstractions of yours—you don't actually *paint* them here?"

"I do when I'm not interrupted," I said pointedly.

"Well, you're risking your life," he declared. "I've seen fire-traps in my time, boychick, but this ain't for real. If I showed it in a picture, they'd say it was overdone." He stuck out a paw. "Harry Hubris," he said. "I guess you've heard of me."

Other than feigning an attack of scrofula, there was no escape now that Vetlugin had crossed me up, so I motioned him in.

He made a quick, beady inventory of the décor. "Go figure it," he said, with a shrug. "It always kills me an artist should hole up in a fleabag to conceive a masterpiece. Still, everybody to their own ulcer. Zuckmayer, I want you to know I consider you one of the nine foremost painters of our time."

"Indeed," I said. "Who are the other eight?"

"Look, pal, don't get me started or I'm liable to talk all night," he said. "I've got maybe the most important collection in the Los Angeles area—five Jackson Pollocks, three Abe Rattners, two of yours—"

"Which ones?"

"I can't remember offhand," he said irritably. "A houseful of paintings, you wouldn't expect me to recall every title. But let's get down to basics. What would you say if I offered you two thousand bucks for an hour's work?"

"I'd be even more suspicious than I am now, which is plenty."

"A blunt answer," he approved. "Well, here's the dodge, and you needn't worry, it's strictly legit. Did you perchance read Irving Stonehenge's biography of John Singer Sargent, *The Tortured Bostonian*?"

I shook my head, and he frowned.

"You're the one guy in America that didn't," he said. "In my humble opinion, it's going to make the greatest documentary-type motion picture since *Lust for Life*. Just visualize Rob Roy Fruitwell in the leading role and tell me how it could miss."

I visualized as best I could, but, never having heard of the man, got nowhere. "Who is he?" I asked.

"Rob Roy?" Hubris's scorn for my ignorance was Olympian. "Only the biggest potential draw in pictures today, that's all," he affirmed. "Properly handled, Fruitwell can be another Kirk Douglas, *and*," he went on, lowering his voice, "I'll breathe you something in strictest confidence. After he has his dimple deepened next spring, you won't be able to tell them apart. My immediate headache, though, and the reason I contacted you, is this. The kid's a born actor and he'll play the hell out of Sargent, but thus far he's appeared exclusively in horse operas—Westerns. What he requires is a little coaching from an expert—a professional artist like you."

"My dear Mr. Hubris," I said. "If you think I can transform a numskull into a master in one lesson—"

"For crisakes, smarten up, will you?" he implored. "All you got to furnish is the pantomime. Show him how to hold a brush, what a palette's for, which end of the tube the color comes out. Remember, this lug don't know, from beauty or the Muse. Two years ago he was a busboy in Fort Wayne."

"But I've never dealt with actors," I objected. "I haven't the faintest clue to their mentality."

"Mentality's one problem you won't have with Rob Roy Fruitwell, brother," Hubris guaranteed. "He's got none. He's just a matzo ball, a sensitized sponge that'll soak up the info you give him and delineate it on the screen."

"Well, I'd have to think it over," I said. "I'm assembling a show at the moment—"

"So your dealer mentioned," he said. "And believe me, Mr. Zuckmayer, I feel like a rat pressuring you, but the point is, we're in a bind. You see, in view of the fact that we start shooting Friday, I had Rob Roy sky in from the Coast last night solely on purpose to huddle with you."

"Then you can jolly well sky him back," I began, and stopped short. After all, if this gasbag was aching to shell out a fat fee for an hour of *expertise*, it'd be downright loony to stand on dignity; my anemic budget could certainly use a transfusion. Obviously sensing I was tempted, Hubris threw in the clincher. Not only would he raise the ante another five hundred, but he was prepared to hand over a check on the spot provided I saw Fruitwell that afternoon. "Well-l-l, all right," I said, overborne. "Have him down here at four o'clock and I'll see what I can do."

"Attaboy!" chortled my caller, whipping out a pen. "You mark my words, Zuckmayer—this may be a turning point in your career. Once the critics dig your name up there in the credits—'Artistic Consultant to the Producer, Harry Hubris'—the whole industry'll be knocking on your door!"

"Don't bother to freeze my blood, please," I said. "Just write out the check."

Hubris made no pretense of concealing his umbrage. "You're a strange apple," he said. "What makes all you artists so anti-social?"

I knew why, but it would have been too expensive to reply. I needed the money.

I was tied up at the framer's after lunch, discussing a new molding of kelp on tinfoil for my show, and didn't get back to the studio until four-fifteen. There was a big rented Cadillac parked outside, the driver of which, a harassed plug-ugly in uniform, was standing off a mob of teenagers screeching and waving autograph books. We had a dandy hassle proving I was kosher, but he finally let me upstairs to the unholy trinity awaiting me. Fruitwell was a standard prize bullock with a Brando tonsure and capped teeth, in a gooseneck sweater under his Italian silk suit which kept riding up to expose his thorax. His agent, a fat little party indistinguishable from a tapir, had apparently been summoned from the hunt, for he wore a Tattersall vest and a deep-skirted hacking coat. The third member of the group, a bearded aesthete dressed entirely in suede, flaunted a whistle on a silver chain encircling his throat. "I'm Dory Gallwise, the assistant director," he introduced himself. "We had to force the lock to get in here. Hope you don't mind."

"Not at all," I said. "Sorry the place is such a pigsty, but—well, you know how bohemians are."

"Oh, it's not so bad," he said graciously. "Of course, as I was just explaining to Rob Roy here, the studio he'll occupy as Sargent will be a lot more imposing. The size of Carnegie Hall, in fact."

"*Natürlich*," I said. "Now, before we commence, Mr. Fruitwell, do you have any questions about art? Anything you'd like me to clarify?"

Immersed in contemplation of a torso on the wall, the young man did not respond at once. Then he lifted his head sleepily. "Yeah, this thing here," he said. " What's it supposed to be—a woman?"

I admitted I had embodied certain female elements, and he snickered.

"You really see that when you look at a dame?" he asked, with a quizzical smile. "Bud, you need therapy. Don't he, Monroe?"

His agent shot me a placatory wink. "Well, I wouldn't go *that* far, Rob Roy," he temporized. "Mr. Zuckmayer reacts to the world around him in a particular way—through the intellect, shall we say? He embodies certain elements—"

"Don't give me that bushwa," the other retorted. "I've dated Mamie van Doren, Marilyn Maxwell, and Diana Dors, and take it from me, pappy, they don't have any corners like that. This moke's in trouble."

"Ha, ha—who isn't?" Gallwise put in with wild gaiety. He cleared his throat nervously. "Listen, boys, let's not hold up Mr. Zuckmayer—he's a busy person." Snapping open his dispatch case, he drew forth a smock and a beret. "Here, Rob Roy, slip these on so you'll get used to the feel of 'em."

"Wait a second," said Fruitwell, clouding over, and wheeled on Monroe. "What the hell are we making, a costume picture? You said I wear a sweat shirt and dungarees."

"In the love scenes, baby," Monroe specified, "but when you're sketching, and like dreaming up your different masterpieces, why, they got to blueprint you're an artist. It establishes your identity."

"Sure, the way a sheriff puts on a tin star," said Gallwise.

"Or a busboy his white coat," I added helpfully.

Fruitwell turned and gave me a long, penetrating look. Then, evidently concluding his ears had deceived him, he surlily donned the habit, and for the next quarter of an hour submitted himself to our charade. I soon perceived that Hubris's depiction of him as a chowderhead was rank flattery. Totally devoid of either co-ordination or the ability to retain, he lumbered about upsetting jars of pigment, gashed himself disastrously with my palette knife, and in a burst of almost inspired clumsiness sprayed fixative into Monroe's eyeball, temporarily blinding the poor wretch. While the latter lay prostrate, whimpering under the poultices with which Gallwise and I rushed to allay his torment, Rob Roy leaned out of the skylight to mollify his fans. Since, however, they had dispersed meanwhile, his largess was wasted, and he was in a distinct pet by the time Monroe was ambulatory.

"You guys through playing beatnik?" he fretted. "Come on, let's blow. If the dauber's got any more dope, he can phone it in to Hubris, or I'll get it from research, on the Coast."

"Rob Roy—honey," pleaded Gallwise. "We'll spring you in two shakes, but just co-operate ten minutes more. I want Mr. Zuckmayer to check on a couple of scenes—you know, to make sure you don't pull a booboo. Here," he said, forcibly planting his charge in a chair. "Run through the situation where Vincent Youmans tries to win you back to your wife."

"Hold on," I protested. "How does *he* come into this?"

"A dramatic license we took to justify the score," he said hurriedly. "He's a young music student at Harvard that Sargent befriends. Can you remember the lines, Rob Roy?"

Fruitwell contorted his forehead in a simulation of deep thought.

"Never mind—spitball some dialogue to give the general idea," said Gallwise. "Go ahead, I'll cue you. I'll be Youmans."

"Hello, Youmans," complied Fruitwell, in a monotone.

"Where you been, man?"

"Oh, just studying my counterpoint over in Cambridge," said Gallwise. "But you certainly are a storm center these days, John Singer. All Beacon Hill is agog the way you threw up your job as stockbroker and abandoned your family. Can a pair of saucy blue orbs underlie this move, as wagging tongues imply?"

Fruitwell uttered a cynical hoot reminiscent of a puppy yelping for a biscuit. "Women!" he scoffed. "I'm tired of those silly little creatures casting their spell on me. I want to paint—to paint, do you hear? I've got to express what I feel deep down inside me! The agony, the heartbreak!"

His agent, who was following the recital from behind a crumpled handkerchief, sprang forward and embraced him. "Lover, don't change a word, a syllable," he begged. "Do that on camera and I personally—Monroe Sweetmeat—promise you an Academy Award. What about it, Mr. Zuckmayer?" he inquired anxiously. "Does it ring true from the artist's point of view?"

"Frighteningly," I agreed. "You've caught the very essence of the creative urge. I have only one criticism." Gallwise stiffened expectantly. "Mr. Fruitwell's got his smock on backwards. The audience might conceivably mistake him for a hairdresser."

"How could they, with that dialogue?" he demanded.

"That's what I mean," I said.

"Well, it's a point to watch," ruminated the director. "Remember that, Rob Roy. Now the key scene, where you get your big break from the hotel manager. The plot point here, Mr. Z., is that Sargent's down and out in New York. It's Christmas Day, the landlord's shut off the gas, and he's starving."

"Tell him about the onion," Monroe giggled.

"A bit of comedy relief," Gallwise explained. "He's so hungry that he finally has to eat this still-life of an onion and a herring."

"What, the canvas itself?" I asked.

"No, no—the objects he's painting," he said impatiently. "Anyway, just at his darkest hour, in comes Tuesday Weld, the coatroom girl at the St. Regis that's been secretly in love with him. She's persuaded the manager to let Sargent paint a mural of King Cole for the men's bar."

"Using the pseudonym of Maxfield Parrish," I supplemented.

"God damn it," burst out Fruitwell, "I've got an eight-man team of writers from the New York *Post* waiting to interview me! Let's do the *scene*!"

Gallwise recoiled as if from a blast furnace. "Uh—on second thought, maybe we don't have to," he stammered, a muscle twitching in his cheek. "I only wanted to corroborate one small detail. Halfway through the action, Mr. Zuckmayer, as Sargent holds Tuesday in his arms, he suddenly stumbles on the idea for his greatest composition, 'The Kiss.' How would a painter react in those circumstances? What exact phraseology would he employ?"

"To herald an inspiration, you mean?" I pondered. "Well, I always smite my forehead and use a simple Greek word—eureka."

Fruitwell ripped off his smock and flung it at his agent. "And for this you fly me from the Coast, you muzzler," he snarled. "Any coffeepot could of told you that!" Suffused with outrage, he stalked to the door, pulverized me and my artifacts with a glance, and was gone. Monroe scampered after him, his face stricken.

Gallwise stood immobilized an instant. Then, swallowing painfully, he folded the smock into the dispatch case like a somnambulist and crossed to the threshold. The crucified smile he turned on me was purest Fra Angelico. "Temperament," he apologized. "But don't be afraid, Mr. Zuckmayer—there won't be a trace of it on the screen. The kid's a great trouper."

It was such nirvana, standing there tranquilly in the dusk after he had left, that I let the phone ring for a full minute. I knew who it was, and my parfait was complete without a Bessarabian cherry, but I also knew Vetlugin's tenacity. I picked up the receiver.

"It's me, Tovarisch." He spoke in such a conspiratorial whisper that for a moment I had trouble distinguishing him. "Look, which painting should I give Mr. Hubris?" he asked breathlessly. "He says he deserves a big one, on account of the publicity you'll get from the film. I claim—"

"I'll settle it." I cut him short. "Call him to the phone."

"But I said you were working—I had orders not to disturb—"

"I've finished," I said. "It's catharsis time."

And it was.

James Thurber

'just about the best thing I ever read'
OGDEN NASH

my life and hard times

PRION HUMOUR CLASSICS

My Life and Hard Times

JAMES THURBER
with an introduction by Clifton Fadiman

"just about the best thing I ever read"
Ogden Nash

My Life and Hard Times is Thurber's greatest work – a surreal slapstick memoir of incidents from Thurber's childhood and college years in Columbus, Ohio, which became an instant bestseller. He narrates in bewildered deadpan the eccentric goings-on of his family and hometown. It is a world full of the absurd anxieties of everyday living. There's the maid, Juanemma, 'who lived in constant dread of being hypnotized'; a mother who believes that electricity leaks out of empty sockets and a mad family mutt called Muggs that bites anything that moves. Add to that unfounded fears about floods, ghosts and burglars, the odd quivering professor and strange uncle and there you have it – an inimitable work of American comic genius. Illustrated by the author.

August 2000
1-85375-397-1
£8.99

The Night the Ghost Got In

The ghost that got into our house on the night of November 17, 1915, raised such a hullabaloo of misunderstandings that I am sorry I didn't just let it keep on walking, and go to bed. Its advent caused my mother to throw a shoe through a window of the house next door and ended up with my grandfather shooting a patrolman. I am sorry, therefore, as I have said, that I ever paid any attention to the footsteps.

They began about a quarter past one o'clock in the morning, a rhythmic, quick-cadenced walking around the dining-room table. My mother was asleep in one room upstairs, my brother Herman in another; grandfather was in the attic, in the old walnut bed which, as you will remember, once fell on my father. I had just stepped out of the bathtub and was busily rubbing myself with a towel when I heard the steps. They were the steps of a man walking rapidly around the dining-room table downstairs. The light from the bathroom shone down the back steps, which dropped directly into the dining-room; I could see the faint shine of plates on the plate-rail; I couldn't see the table. The steps kept going round and round the table; at regular intervals a board creaked, when it was trod upon. I supposed at first that it was my father or my brother Roy, who had gone to Indianapolis but were expected home at any time. I suspected next that it was a burglar. It did not enter my mind until later that it was a ghost.

After the walking had gone on for perhaps three minutes, I tiptoed to Herman's room. 'Psst!' I hissed, in the dark, shaking him. 'Awp,' he said, in the low, hopeless tone of a despondent beagle—he always half suspected that something would 'get him' in the night. I told him who I was. 'There's something downstairs!' I said. He got up and followed me to the head of the back staircase. We listened together. There was no sound. The steps had ceased. Herman looked at me in some alarm: I had only the bath towel around my waist. He wanted to go back to bed, but I gripped his arm. 'There's something down there!' I said. Instantly the steps began again, circled the dining-room table like a man running, and started up the stairs toward us, heavily, two at a time. The light still shone palely down the stairs; we saw nothing coming; we only heard the steps. Herman rushed to his room and slammed the door. I slammed shut the door at the stairs top and held my knee against it. After a long minute, I slowly opened it again. There was nothing there. There was no sound. None of us ever heard the ghost again.

The slamming of the doors had aroused mother: she peered out of her room. 'What on earth are you boys doing?' she demanded. Herman ventured out of his room. 'Nothing,' he said, gruffly, but he was, in colour, a light green. 'What was all that running around downstairs?' said mother. So she had heard the steps, too! We just looked at her. 'Burglars!' she shouted, intuitively. I tried to quiet her by starting lightly downstairs.

'Come on, Herman,' I said.

'I'll stay with mother,' he said. 'She's all excited.'

I stepped back onto the landing.

'Don't either of you go a step,' said mother. 'We'll call the police.' Since the phone was downstairs, I didn't see how we were going to call the police—nor did I want the police—but mother made one of her quick, incomparable decisions. She flung up a window of her bedroom which faced the bedroom windows of the house of a neighbour, picked up a shoe, and whammed it through a pane of glass across the narrow space that separated the two houses. Glass tinkled into the bedroom occupied by a retired engraver named Bodwell and his wife. Bodwell had been for some years in rather a bad way and was subject to mild 'attacks'. Most everybody we knew or lived near had *some* kind of attacks.

It was now about two o'clock of a moonless night; clouds hung black and low. Bodwell was at the window in a minute, shouting, frothing a little, shaking his fist. 'We'll sell the house and go back to Peoria' we could hear Mrs Bodwell saying. It was some time before Mother 'got through' to Bodwell. 'Burglars!' she shouted. 'Burglars in the house!' Herman and I hadn't dared to tell her that it was not burglars but ghosts, for she was even more afraid of ghosts than of burglars. Bodwell at first thought that she meant there were burglars in his house, but finally he quieted down and called the police for us over an extension phone by his bed. After he had disappeared from the window, mother suddenly made as if to throw another shoe, not because there was further need of it but, as she later explained, because the thrill of heaving a shoe through a window glass had enormously taken her fancy. I prevented her.

The police were on hand in a commendably short time: a Ford sedan full of them, two on motorcycles, and a patrol wagon with about eight in it and a few reporters. They began banging at our front door. Flashlights shot streaks of gleam up and down the walls, across the yard, down the walk between our house and Bodwell's. 'Open up!' cried a hoarse voice. 'We're men from Headquarters!' I wanted to go down and let them in, since there they were, but mother wouldn't hear of it. 'You haven't a stitch on,' she pointed out. 'You'd catch your death.' I wound the towel around me again. Finally the cops put their shoulders to our big heavy front door with its thick bevelled glass and broke it in: I could hear a rending of wood and a splash of glass on the floor of the hall. Their lights played all over the living-room and criss-crossed nervously in the dining-room, stabbed into hallways, shot up the front stairs and finally up the back. They caught me standing in my towel at the top. A heavy policeman bounded up the steps. 'Who are you?' he demanded. 'I live here,' I said. 'Well, whattsa matta, ya hot?' he asked. It was, as a matter of fact, cold; I went to my room and pulled on some trousers. On my way out, a cop stuck a gun into my ribs. 'Whatta you doin' here?' he demanded. 'I live here,' I said.

The officer in charge reported to mother. 'No sign of nobody, lady,' he said. 'Musta got away—what'd he look like?' 'There were two or three of them,' mother said, 'whooping and carrying on and slamming doors.' 'Funny,' said the cop. 'All ya windows and doors was locked on the inside tight as a tick.'

Downstairs, we could hear the tramping of the other police. Police were all over the place; doors were yanked open, drawers were yanked open, windows were shot up and pulled down, furniture fell with dull thumps. A half-dozen policemen emerged out of the darkness of the front hallway upstairs. They began to ransack the floor: pulled beds away from walls, tore clothes off hooks in the closets, pulled suit-cases and boxes off shelves. One of them found an old zither that Roy had won in a pool tournament. 'Looky here, Joe,' he said, strumming it with a big paw. The cop named Joe took it and turned it over. 'What is it?' he asked me. 'It's an old zither our guinea pig used to sleep on,' I said. It was true that a pet guinea pig we once had would never sleep anywhere except on the zither, but I should never have said so. Joe and the other cop looked at me a long time. They put the zither back on a shelf.

'No sign o' nuthin',' said the cop who had first spoken to mother. 'This guy,' he explained to the others, jerking a thumb at me, 'was nekked. The lady seems historical.' They all nodded, but said nothing; just looked at me. In the small silence we all heard a creaking in the attic. Grandfather was turning over in bed. 'What's 'at?' snapped Joe. Five or six cops sprang for the attic door before I could intervene or explain. I realized that it would be bad if they burst in on grandfather unannounced, or even announced. He was going through a phase in which he believed that General Meade's men, under steady hammering by Stonewall Jackson, were beginning to retreat and even desert.

When I got to the attic, things were pretty confused. Grandfather had evidently jumped to the conclusion that the police were deserters from Meade's army, trying to hide away in his attic. He bounded out of bed wearing a long flannel night-gown over long woollen underwear, a night-cap, and a leather jacket around his chest. The cops must have realized at once that the indignant white-haired old man belonged in the house, but they had no chance to say so. 'Back, ye cowardly dogs!' roared grandfather. 'Back t' the lines, ye goddam lily-livered cattle!' With that, he fetched the officer who found the zither a flat-handed smack alongside his head that sent him sprawling. The others beat a retreat, but not fast enough; grandfather grabbed Zither's gun from its holster and let fly. The report seemed to crack the rafters; smoke filled the attic. A cop cursed and shot his hand to his shoulder. Somehow, we all finally got downstairs again and locked the door against the old gentleman. He fired once or twice more in the darkness and then went back to bed. 'That was grandfather,' I explained to Joe, out of breath. 'He thinks you're deserters.' 'I'll say he does,' said Joe.

The cops were reluctant to leave without getting their hands on somebody besides grandfather; the night had been distinctly a defeat for them. Furthermore, they obviously didn't like the 'layout'; something looked—and I can see their viewpoint—phony. They began to poke into things again. A reporter, a thin-faced, wispy man, came up to me. I had put on one of mother's blouses, not being able to find anything else. The reporter looked at me with mingled suspicion and interest. 'Just what the hell is the real lowdown here, Bud?' he asked. I decided to be frank with him. 'We had ghosts,' I said. He gazed at me a long time as if I were a slot machine into which he had, without results, dropped a nickel. Then he walked away. The cops followed him, the one grandfather shot holding his now-bandaged arm, cursing and blaspheming. 'I'm gonna get my gun back from that old bird,' said the zither-cop. 'Yeh,' said Joe. 'You—and who else?' I told them I would bring it to the station house the next day.

'What was the matter with that one policeman?' mother asked, after they had gone. 'Grandfather shot him,' I said. 'What for?' she demanded. I told her he was a deserter. 'Of all things!' said mother. 'He was such a nice-looking young man.'

Grandfather was fresh as a daisy and full of jokes at breakfast next morning. We thought at first he had forgotten all about what had happened, but he hadn't. Over his third cup of coffee, he glared at Herman and me. 'What was the idee of all them cops tarryhootin' round the house last night?' he demanded. He had us there.

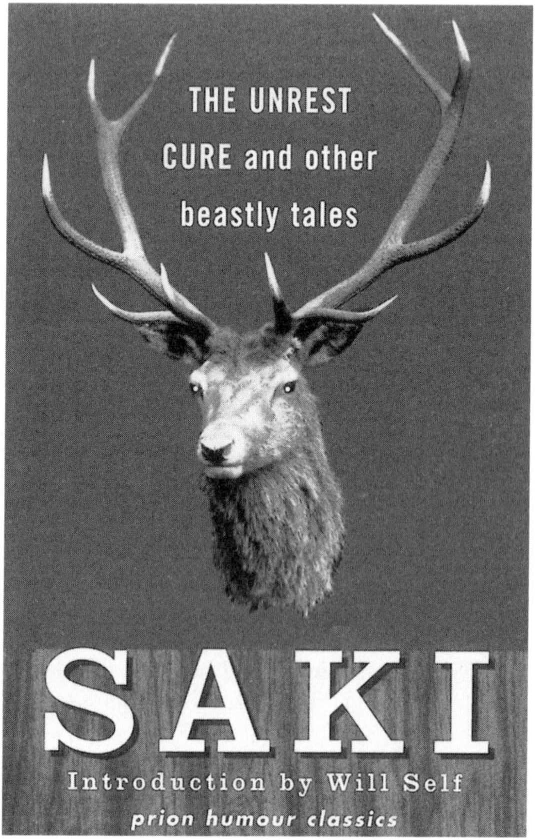
THE UNREST
CURE and other
beastly tales
SAKI
Introduction by Will Self
prion humour classics

The Unrest-Cure

AND OTHER BEASTLY TALES

SAKI

with a new introduction by Will Self

"they dazzle and delight"

Graham Greene

Take a decent helping of P G Wodehouse – aunts, country manors and all – a soupçon of Wilde's epigrammatic wit, season with the bloodthirsty malevolence of Edward Lear and Roald Dahl, and you will have an idea of the inimitable genius of Hector Hugh Munro, alias Saki.

This collection gathers together for the first time the cream of Saki's flawlessly-etched cautionary tales in which a gleeful and predatory Nature is always waiting to claim its next victim, where upper-class twits meet with fittingly macabre accidents, where children are invariably beastly, and his mischievous young heroes, like Clovis Sangrail and Reginald, get the better of their peers using barbed sarcasm and magical hoaxes involving everything from black magic to genocide.

May 2000
1-85375-370-X
£8.99

The Unrest-Cure

On the rack in the railway carriage immediately opposite Clovis was a solidly wrought travelling bag, with a carefully written label, on which was inscribed, "J. P. Huddle, The Warren, Tilfield, near Slowborough." Immediately below the rack sat the human embodiment of the label, a solid, sedate individual, sedately dressed, sedately conversational. Even without his conversation (which was addressed to a friend seated by his side, and touched chiefly on such topics as the backwardness of Roman hyacinths and the prevalence of measles at the Rectory), one could have gauged fairly accurately the temperament and mental outlook of the travelling bag's owner. But he seemed unwilling to leave anything to the imagination of a casual observer, and his talk grew presently personal and introspective.

"I don't know how it is," he told his friend, "I'm not much over forty, but I seem to have settled down into a deep groove of elderly middle age. My sister shows the same tendency. We like everything to be exactly in its accustomed place; we like things to happen exactly at their appointed times; we like everything to be usual, orderly, punctual, methodical, to a hair's breadth, to a minute. It distresses and upsets us if it is not so. For instance, to take a very trifling matter, a thrush has built its nest year after year in the catkin-tree on the lawn; this year, for no obvious reason, it is building in the ivy on the garden wall. We have said very little about it, but I think we both feel that the change is unnecessary, and just a little irritating."

"Perhaps," said the friend, "it is a different thrush."

"We have suspected that," said J. P. Huddle, "and I think it gives us even more cause for annoyance. We don't feel that we want a change of thrush at our time of life; and yet, as I have said, we have scarcely reached an age when these things should make themselves seriously felt."

"What you want," said the friend, "is an Unrest-cure."

"An Unrest-cure? I've never heard of such a thing."

"You've heard of Rest-cures for people who've broken down under stress of too much worry and strenuous living; well, you're suffering from overmuch repose and placidity, and you need the opposite kind of treatment."

"But where would one go for such a thing?"

"Well, you might stand as an Orange candidate for Kilkenny, or do a course of district visiting in one of the Apache quarters of Paris, or give lectures in Berlin to prove that most of Wagner's music was written by Gambetta; and there's always the interior of Morocco to travel in. But, to be really effective, the Unrest-cure ought to be tried in the home. How you would do it I haven't the faintest idea."

It was at this point in the conversation that Clovis became galvanized into alert attention. After all, his two days' visit to an elderly relative at Slowborough did not promise much excitement. Before the train had stopped he had decorated his sinister shirt-cuff with the inscription, "J. P. Huddle, The Warren, Tilfield, near Slowborough."

Two mornings later Mr. Huddle broke in on his sister's privacy as she sat reading *Country Life* in the morning room. It was her day and hour and place for reading *Country Life*, and the intrusion was absolutely irregular; but he bore in his hand a telegram, and in that household telegrams were recognized as happening by the hand of God. This particular telegram partook of the nature of a thunderbolt. "Bishop examining confirmation class in neighbourhood unable stay rectory on account measles invokes your hospitality sending secretary arrange."

"I scarcely know the Bishop; I've only spoken to him once," exclaimed J. P. Huddle, with the exculpating air of one who realizes too late the indiscretion of speaking to strange Bishops. Miss Huddle was the first to rally; she disliked thunderbolts as fervently as her brother did, but the womanly instinct in her told her that thunderbolts must be fed.

"We can curry the cold duck," she said. It was not the appointed day for curry, but the little orange envelope involved a certain departure from rule and custom. Her brother said nothing, but his eyes thanked her for being brave.

"A young gentleman to see you," announced the parlourmaid.

"The secretary!" murmured the Huddles in unison; they instantly stiffened into a demeanour which proclaimed that, though they held all strangers to be guilty, they were willing to hear anything they might have to say in their defence. The young gentleman, who came into the room with a certain elegant haughtiness, was not at all Huddle's idea of a bishop's secretary; he had not supposed that the episcopal establishment could have afforded such an expensively upholstered article when there were so many other claims on its resources. The face was fleetingly familiar; if he had bestowed more attention on the fellow-traveller sitting opposite him in the railway carriage two days before he might have recognized Clovis in his present visitor.

"You are the Bishop's secretary?" asked Huddle, becoming consciously deferential.

"His confidential secretary," answered Clovis. "You may call me Stanislaus; my other name doesn't matter. The Bishop and Colonel Alberti may be here to lunch. I shall be here in any case."

It sounded rather like the programme of a Royal visit.

"The Bishop is examining a confirmation class in the neighbourhood, isn't he?" asked Miss Huddle.

"Ostensibly," was the dark reply, followed by a request for a large-scale map of the locality.

Clovis was still immersed in a seemingly profound study of the map when another telegram arrived. It was addressed to "Prince Stanislaus, care of Huddle, The Warren, etc." Clovis glanced at the contents and announced: "The Bishop and Alberti won't be here till late in the afternoon." Then he returned to his scrutiny of the map.

The luncheon was not a very festive function. The princely secretary ate and drank with fair appetite, but severely discouraged conversation. At the finish of the meal he broke suddenly into a radiant smile, thanked his hostess for a charming repast, and kissed her hand with deferential rapture. Miss Huddle was unable to decide in her mind whether the action savoured of Louis Quatorzian courtliness or the reprehensible Roman attitude towards the Sabine women. It was not her day for having a headache, but she felt that the circumstances excused her, and retired to her room to have as much headache as was possible before the Bishop's arrival. Clovis, having asked the way to the nearest telegraph office, disappeared presently down the carriage drive. Mr. Huddle met him in the hall some two hours later, and asked when the Bishop would arrive.

"He is in the library with Alberti," was the reply.

"But why wasn't I told? I never knew he had come!" exclaimed Huddle.

"No one knows he is here," said Clovis; "the quieter we can keep matters the better. And on no account disturb him in the library. Those are his orders."

"But what is all this mystery about? And who is Alberti? And isn't the Bishop going to have tea?"

"The Bishop is out for blood, not tea."

"Blood!" gasped Huddle, who did not find that the thunderbolt improved on acquaintance.

"Tonight is going to be a great night in the history of Christendom," said Clovis. "We are going to massacre every Jew in the neighbourhood."

"To massacre the Jews!" said Huddle indignantly. "Do you mean to tell me there's a general rising against them?"

"No, it's the Bishop's own idea. He's in there arranging all the details now."

"But—the Bishop is such a tolerant, humane man."

"That is precisely what will heighten the effect of his action. The sensation will be enormous."

That at least Huddle could believe.

"He will be hanged!" he exclaimed with conviction.

"A motor is waiting to carry him to the coast, where a steam yacht is in readiness."

"But there aren't thirty Jews in the whole neighbourhood," protested Huddle, whose brain, under the repeated shocks of the day, was operating with the uncertainty of a telegraph wire during earthquake disturbances.

"We have twenty-six on our list," said Clovis, referring to a bundle of notes. "We shall be able to deal with them all the more thoroughly."

"Do you mean to tell me that you are meditating violence against a man like Sir Leon Birberry," stammered Huddle; "he's one of the most respected men in the country."

"He's down on our list," said Clovis carelessly; "after all, we've got men we can trust to do our job, so we shan't have to rely on local assistance. And we've got some Boy Scouts helping us as auxiliaries."

"Boy Scouts!"

"Yes; when they understood there was real killing to be done they were even keener than the men."

"This thing will be a blot on the Twentieth Century!"

"And your house will be the blotting-pad. Have you realized that half the papers of Europe and the United States will publish pictures of it? By the way, I've sent some photographs of you and your sister, that I found in the library, to the *Martin* and *Die Woche*; I hope you don't mind. Also a sketch of the staircase; most of the killing will probably be done on the staircase."

The emotions that were surging in J. P. Huddle's brain were almost too intense to be disclosed in speech, but he managed to gasp out: "There aren't any Jews in this house."

"Not at present," said Clovis.

"I shall go to the police," shouted Huddle with sudden energy.

"In the shrubbery," said Clovis, "are posted ten men, who have orders to fire on any one who leaves the house without my signal of permission. Another armed picquet is in ambush near the front gate. The Boy Scouts watch the back premises."

At this moment the cheerful hoot of a motor-horn was heard from the drive. Huddle rushed to the hall door with the feeling of a man half-awakened from a nightmare, and beheld Sir Leon Birberry, who had driven himself over in his car. "I got your telegram," he said; "what's up?"

Telegram? It seemed to be a day of telegrams.

"Come here at once. Urgent. James Huddle," was the purport of the message displayed before Huddle's bewildered eyes.

"I see it all!" he exclaimed suddenly in a voice shaken with agitation, and with a look of agony in the direction of the shrubbery he hauled the astonished Birberry into the house. Tea had just been laid in the hall, but the now thoroughly panic-stricken Huddle dragged his protesting guest upstairs, and in a few minutes' time the entire household had been summoned to that region of momentary safety. Clovis alone graced the tea-table with his presence; the fanatics in the library were evidently too immersed in their monstrous machinations to dally with the solace of teacup and hot toast. Once the youth rose, in answer to the summons of the front-door bell, and admitted Mr. Paul Isaacs, shoemaker and parish councillor, who had also received a pressing invitation to The Warren. With an atrocious assumption of courtesy, which a Borgia could hardly have outdone, the secretary escorted this new captive of his net to the head of the stairway, where his involuntary host awaited him.

And then ensued a long ghastly vigil of watching and waiting. Once or twice Clovis left the house to stroll across to the shrubbery, returning always to the library, for the purpose evidently of making a brief report. Once he took in the letters from the evening postman, and brought them to the top of the stairs with punctilious politeness. After his next absence he came half-way up the stairs to make an announcement.

"The Boy Scouts mistook my signal, and have killed the postman. I've had very little practice in this sort of thing, you see. Another time I shall do better."

The housemaid, who was engaged to be married to the evening postman, gave way to clamorous grief.

"Remember that your mistress has a headache," said J. P. Huddle. (Miss Huddle's headache was worse.)

Clovis hastened downstairs, and after a short visit to the library returned with another message:

"The Bishop is sorry to hear that Miss Huddle has a headache. He is issuing orders that as far as possible no firearms shall be used near the house; any killing that is necessary on the premises will be done with cold steel. The Bishop does not see why a man should not be a gentleman as well as a Christian."

That was the last they saw of Clovis; it was nearly seven o'clock, and his elderly relative liked him to dress for dinner. But, though he had left them for ever, the lurking suggestion of his presence haunted the lower regions of the house during the long hours of the wakeful night, and every creak of the stairway, every rustle of wind through the shrubbery, was fraught with horrible meaning. At about seven next morning the gardener's boy and the early postman finally convinced the watchers that the Twentieth Century was still unblotted.

"I don't suppose," mused Clovis, as an early train bore him townwards, "that they will be in the least grateful for the Unrest-cure."

The papers of A.J.
Wentworth, BA
H F Ellis
"ONE OF THE FUNNIEST BOOKS EVER"
Sunday Express

The Papers of A J Wentworth BA

H F ELLIS

with a new introduction by Miles Kington

"one of the funniest books ever"

Sunday Express

Close to retirement, A J Wentworth, though well-intentioned, is a humourless, ineffective educator of the old school. Despite an unshakeable faith in his own methods, he is ill-equipped to deal with the devious vagaries of the modern schoolboy. While he fusses over trivialities and stickles over rules, the pupils of Set IIIA quietly run riotous circles around him, especially the boy Mason. His fellow masters aren't above exploiting his gullibility and pomposity for their own amusement either. If this wasn't enough Wentworth is prone to frequent mishaps which regularly lead him into all kinds of hot water. Yet Wentworth is determined to hold his head high and live in cheerful denial of the absurd hand life seems to constantly deal him.

September 2000
1-85375-398-X
£8.99

Statement of Arthur James Wentworth BA

My name is Arthur James Wentworth, I am unmarried and I am by profession an assistant master at Burgrove Preparatory School, Wilminster. The Headmaster is the Reverend Gregory Saunders, M.A. He is known to the boys as the Squid—not necessarily, I think, a term of opprobrium. He is a classical scholar of moderate attainments, a generous employer and much given to the use of the expression, 'The School must come first, Wentworth.' I attach no particular meaning to this remark.

At 11.15 on the morning of Saturday 8 July, I entered Classroom 4 for the purpose of instructing Set IIIA in Algebra. There were present Anderson, Atkins, Clarke, Etheridge, Hillman, Hopgood II, Mason, Otterway, Sapoulos, Trench and Willliamson. Heathcote, who has, I am told, a boil, was absent. It should be explained that though I have given these names in the alphabetical order in which they appear in the school list, that is not the order in which the boys were sitting on this occasion. It is the custom at Burgrove for boys to sit according to their position in the previous week's mark-lists. Thus in the front row were seated Etheridge, a most promising mathematician, Hillman, Mason, Otterway and Clarke. Hopgood II, the boy whom I am now accused of assaulting, was in the middle of the second row. The third and last row was shared by Sapoulos, a Greek, and Atkins, a cretin. I do not think these facts have any bearing on anything that is to follow, but I give them for the sake of completeness.'

'This morning,' I remarked, taking up my *Hall and Knight*, 'we will do problems,' and I told them at once that if there was any more of that groaning they would do nothing but problems for the next month. It is my experience, as an assistant master of some years' standing, that if groaning is not checked immediately it may swell to enormous proportions. I make it my business to stamp on it.

Mason, a fair-haired boy with glasses, remarked when the groaning had died down that it would not be possible to do problems for the next month, and on being asked why not, replied that there were only three weeks more of term. This was true, and I decided to make no reply. He then asked if he could have a mark for that. I said, 'No, Mason, you may not,' and, taking up my book and a piece of chalk, read out, 'I am just half as old as my father and in twenty years I shall be five years older than he was twenty years ago. How old am I?' Atkins promptly replied, 'Forty-two.' I inquired of him how, unless he was gifted with supernatural powers, he imagined he could produce the answer without troubling to do any Working-Out. He said, 'I saw it in the *Schools Year-book*.' This stupid reply caused a great deal of laughter, which I suppressed.

I should have spoken sharply to Atkins, but at this moment I noticed that his neighbour Sapoulos, the Greek boy, appeared to be eating toffee, a practice which is forbidden at Burgrove during school hours. I ordered him to stand up. 'Sapoulos,' I said, 'you are not perhaps quite used yet to our English ways, and I shall not punish you this time for your disobedience; but please understand that I will not have eating in my class. You did not come here to eat but to learn. If you try hard and pay attention,

I do not altogether despair of teaching you something, but if you do not wish to learn I cannot help you. You might as well go back to your own country.' Mason, without being given permission to speak, cried excitedly, 'He can't, sir. Didn't you know? His father was chased out of Greece in a revolution or something. A big man with a black beard chased him for three miles and he had to escape in a small boat. It's true, sir. You ask him. Sapoulos got hit on the knee with a brick, didn't you, Sappy? And his grandmother—at least I think it was his grandmother—'

'That will do, Mason,' I said. 'Who threw that?'

I am not, I hope, a martinet, but I will not tolerate the throwing of paper darts, or other missiles in my algebra set. Some of the boys make small pellets out of their blotting-paper and flick them with their garters. This sort of thing has to be put down with a firm hand or work becomes impossible. I accordingly warned the boy responsible that another offence would mean an imposition. He had the impertinence to ask what sort of an imposition. I said that it would be a pretty stiff imposition, and if he wished to know more exact details he had only to throw another dart to find out. He thereupon threw another dart.

I confess that at this I lost patience and threatened to keep the whole set in during the afternoon if I had any more trouble. The lesson then proceeded.

It was not until I had completed my working out of the problem on the board that I realized I had worked on the assumption—of course ridiculous —that I was *twice* my father's age instead of *half*. This gave the false figure of minus 90 for my own age. Some boy said, 'Crikey!' I at once whipped round and demanded to know who had spoken. Otterway suggested that it might have been Hopgood II talking in his sleep. I was about to reprimand Otterway for impertinence when I realized that Hopgood actually was asleep and had in fact, according to Williamson, been asleep since the beginning of the period. Mason said, 'He hasn't missed much, anyway.'

I then threw my *Hall and Knight*. It has been suggested that it was intended to hit Hopgood II. This is false. I never wake up sleeping boys by throwing books at them, as hundreds of old Burgrove boys will be able to testify. I intended to hit Mason, and it was by a mischance which I shall always regret that Hopgood was struck. I have had, as I told my Headmaster, a great deal to put up with from Mason, and no one who knows the boy blames me for the attempt to do him some physical violence. It is indeed an accepted maxim, in the Common Room that physical violence is the only method of dealing with Mason which produces any results; to this the Headmaster some time ago added a rider that the boy be instructed to remove his spectacles before being assaulted. That I forgot to do this must be put down to the natural agitation of a mathematics master caught out in an error. But I blame myself for it.

I do not blame myself for the unfortunate stunning of Hopgood II. It was an accident. I did all I could for the boy when it was discovered (I think by Etheridge) that he had been rendered unconscious. I immediately summoned the Headmaster and we talked the matter over. We agreed that concealment was impossible and that I must give a full account of the circumstances to the police. Meanwhile the work of the school was to go on as usual; Hopgood himself would have wished it. The Headmaster added that in any case the School must come first.

I have made this statement after being duly cautioned, of my own free will and in the presence of witnesses. I have read it through three times with considerable satisfaction, and am prepared to state on oath that it is a true and full account of the circumstances leading up to the accident to Hopgood II. I wish only to add that the boy is now none the worse for the blow, and has indeed shown increased zeal for his studies since the occurrence.

(*Signed*) A. J. Wentworth BA

July 1939

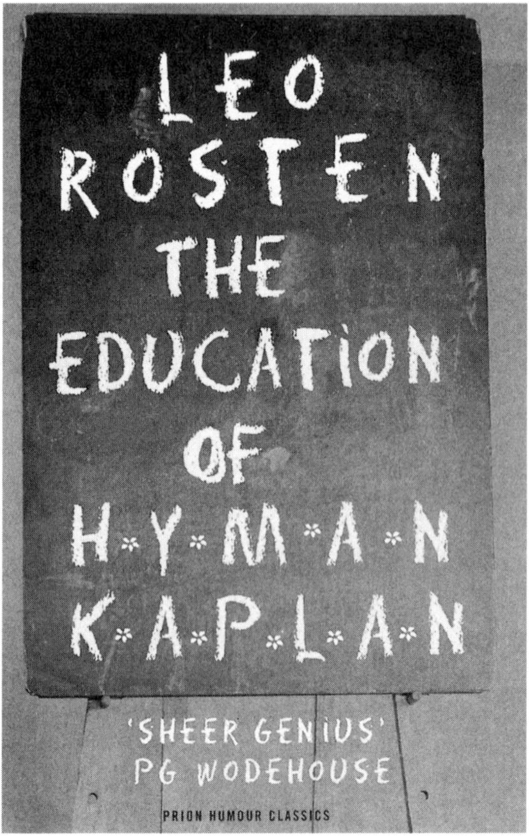
LEO
ROSTEN
THE
EDUCATION
OF
H·Y·M·A·N
K·A·P·L·A·N
'SHEER GENIUS'
PG WODEHOUSE
PRION HUMOUR CLASSICS

THE EDUCATION OF H*Y*M*A*N K*A*P*L*A*N

LEO ROSTEN

with a new introduction by HOWARD JACOBSON

"sheer genius"
P G Wodehouse

In the beginner's grade at New York's American Preparatory Night School for Adults, the struggle between the long suffering teacher Mr Parkhill and his eager yet hapless immigrant pupils is a perpetual comedy of linguistic error and verbal indiscretion. By far the most ebullient pupil is Hyman Kaplan, who, with his proud, beneficent smile and whispered remarks, slowly drives 'Mr Pockheel' to the end of his resources. Despite his enthusiasm, Mr Kaplan never quite grasps the fundamental principles, yet his mind works with its own inimitable logic that enables him to emerge triumphant from any predicament, lending him a touch of warped genius. The stories first appeared in *The New Yorker* and were collected in 1937 as *The Education of Hyman Kaplan* – a perennial comic classic that has never been out of print in America.

May 2000
1-85375-382-3
£8.99

Mr K*A*P*L*A*N, *the Comparative and the Superlative*

For two weeks Mr. Parkhill had been delaying the inescapable: Mr. Kaplan, like the other students in the beginners' grade of the American Night Preparatory School for Adults, would have to present a composition for class analysis. All the students had had their turn writing the assignment on the board, a composition of one hundred words, entitled "My Job." Now only Mr. Kaplan's rendition remained.

It would be more accurate to say Mr. K*A*P*L*A*N's rendition of the assignment remained, for even in thinking of that distinguished student, Mr. Parkhill saw the image of his unmistakable signature, in all its red-blue-green glory. The multicolored characters were more than a trademark; they were an assertion of individuality, a symbol of singularity, a proud expression of Mr. Kaplan's Inner Self. To Mr. Parkhill, the signature took on added meaning because it was associated with the man who had said his youthful ambition had been to become "a physician and sergeant," the Titan who had declined the verb "to fail": "fail, failed, bankropt."

One night, after the two weeks' procrastination, Mr. Parkhill decided to face the worst. "Mr. Kaplan, I think it's your turn to—er—write your composition on the board."

Mr. Kaplan's great, buoyant smile grew more great and more buoyant. "My!" he exclaimed. He rose, looked around at the class proudly as if surveying the blessed who were to witness a linguistic *tour de force*, stumbled over Mrs. Moskowitz's feet with a polite "Vould you be so kindly?" and took his place at the blackboard. There he rejected several pieces of chalk critically, nodded to Mr. Parkhill—it was a nod of distinct reassurance—and then printed in firm letters:

My Job A Cotter In Dress Faktory
Comp. by
H*Y*

"You need not write your name on the board," interrupted Mr. Parkhill quickly. "Er—to save time..."

Mr. Kaplan's face expressed astonishment. "Podden me, Mr. Pockheel. But de name is by me *pot* of mine composition."

"Your name is *part* of the composition?" asked Mr. Parkhill in an anxious tone.

"Yas*sir*!" said Mr. Kaplan with dignity. He printed the rest of H*Y*M*A*N K*A*P*L*A*N for all to see and admire. You could tell it was a disappointment for him not to have colored chalk for this performance. In pale white the elegance of his work was dissipated. The name, indeed, seemed unreal, the letters stark, anemic, almost denuded.

His brow wrinkled and perspiring, Mr. Kaplan wrote the saga of A Cotter In Dress Faktory on the board, with much scratching of the chalk and an undertone of sound. Mr. Kaplan repeated each word to himself softly, as if trying to give to its spelling some of the flavor and originality of his pronunciation. The smile on the face of Mr.

Kaplan had taken on something beatific and imperishable: it was his first experience at the blackboard; it was his moment of glory. He seemed to be writing more slowly than necessary as if to prolong the ecstasy of his Hour. When he had finished he said "Hau Kay" with distinct regret in his voice, and sat down. Mr. Parkhill observed the composition in all its strange beauty:

My Job A Cotter In Dress Faktory
Comp. by
H*Y*M*A*N K*A*P*L*A*N

Shakspere is saying what fulls man is and I am feeling just the same way when I am thinking about mine job a cotter in Dress Faktory on 38 st. by 7 av. For why should we slafing in dark place by laktric lights and all kinds hot for $30 or maybe $36 with overtime, for Boss who is fat and driving in fency automobil? I ask! Because we are the deprassed workers of world. And are being exployted. By Bosses. In mine shop is no difference. Oh how bad is laktric light, oh how is all kinds hot. And when I am telling Foreman should be better conditions he hollers, Kaplan you redical!!

At this point a glazed look came into Mr. Parkhill's eyes, but he read on.

So I keep still and work by bad light and always hot. But somday will the workers making Bosses work! And then Kaplan will give to them bad laktric and positively no windows for the air should come in! So they can know what it means to slafe! Kaplan will make Foreman a cotter like he is. And give the most bad dezigns to cot out. Justice.

Mine job is cotting Dress dezigns.

T-H-E E-N-D

Mr. Parkhill read the amazing document over again. His eyes, glazed but a moment before, were haunted now. It was true: spelling, diction, sentence structure, punctuation, capitalization, the use of the present perfect for the present—all true.

"Is planty mistakes, I s'pose," suggested Mr. Kaplan modestly.

"Y-yes...yes, there are many mistakes."

"Dat's because I'm tryink to give *dip ideas*," said Mr. Kaplan with the sigh of those who storm heaven.

Mr. Parkhill girded his mental loins. "Mr. Kaplan—er—your composition doesn't really meet the assignment. You haven't described your *job*, what you *do*, what your work is."

"Vell, it's not soch a interastink jop," said Mr. Kaplan.

"Your composition is not a simple exposition. It's more of a—well, an *essay* on your *attitude*."

"Oh, fine!" cried Mr. Kaplan with enthusiasm.

"No, no," said Mr. Parkhill hastily. "The assignment was *meant* to be a composition. You see, we must begin with simple exercises before we try—er—more philosophical essays."

Mr. Kaplan nodded with resignation. "So naxt time should be no ideas, like abot Shaksbeer? Should be only *fects*?"

"Y-yes. No ideas, only—er—facts."

You could see by Mr. Kaplan's martyred smile that his wings, like those of an eagle, were being clipped.

"And Mr. Kaplan—er—why do you use 'Kaplan' in the body of your composition? Why don't you say '*I* will make the foreman a cutter' instead of '*Kaplan* will make the foreman a cutter'?"

Mr. Kaplan's response was instantaneous. "I'm so glad you eskink me dis! Ha! I'm usink 'Keplen' in de composition for plain and tsimple rizzon: becawss I didn't vant de reader should tink I am *prajudiced* against de foreman, so I said it more like abot a strenger: '*Keplen* vill make de foreman a cotter!' "

In the face of this subtle passion for objectivity, Mr. Parkhill was silent. He called for corrections. A forest of hands went up. Miss Mitnick pointed out errors in spelling, the use of capital letters, punctuation; Mr. Norman Bloom corrected several more words, rearranged sentences, and said, "Woikers is exployted with an '*i*,' not 'y' as Kaplan makes"; Miss Caravello changed "fulls" to "fools," and declared herself uncertain as to the validity of the word "Justice" standing by itself in "da smalla da sentence"; Mr. Sam Pinsky said he was sure Mr. Kaplan meant "*opprassed* voikers of de voild, not *deprassed*, aldough dey are deprassed *too*," to which Mr. Kaplan replied, "So ve bote got right, no? Don' *chenge* 'deprassed,' only *add* 'opprassed.' "

Then Mr. Parkhill went ahead with his own corrections, changing tenses, substituting prepositions, adding the definite article. Through the whole barrage Mr. Kaplan kept shaking his head, murmuring "Mine gootness!" each time a correction was made. But he smiled all the while. He seemed to be proud of the very number of errors he had made; of the labor to which the class was being forced in his service; of the fact that his *ideas*, his creation, could survive so concerted an onslaught. And as the composition took more respectable form, Mr. Kaplan's smile grew more expansive.

"Now, class," said Mr. Parkhill, "I want to spend a few minutes explaining something about adjectives. Mr. Kaplan uses the phrase—er—'most bad.' That's wrong. There is a word for 'most bad.' It is what we call the superlative form of 'bad.'" Mr. Parkhill explained the use of the positive, comparative, and superlative forms of the adjective. "'Tall, taller, tallest.' 'Rich, richer, richest.' Is that clear? Well then, let us try a few others."

The class took up the game with enthusiasm. Miss Mitnick submitted "dark, darker, darkest"; Mr. Scymzak, "fat, fatter, fattest."

"But there are certain exceptions to this general form," Mr. Parkhill went on. The class, which had long ago learned to respect that gamin, The Exception to the Rule, nodded solemnly. "For instance, we don't say 'good, gooder, goodest,' do we?"

"No, sir!" cried Mr. Kaplan impetuously. "'Good, gooder, good*est*?' Ha! It's to leff!"

"We say that X, for example, is good. Y, however, is—?" Mr. Parkhill arched an eyebrow interrogatively.

"Batter!" said Mr. Kaplan.

"Right! And Z is—?"

"High-cless!"

Mr. Parkhill's eyebrow dropped. "No," he said sadly.

"*Not* high-cless?" asked Mr. Kaplan incredulously. For him there was no word more superlative.

"No, Mr. Kaplan, the word is 'best.' And the word 'bad,' of which you tried to use the superlative form...It isn't *bad, badder, baddest.*' It's 'bad'…and what's the comparative? Anyone?"

"Worse," volunteered Mr. Bloom.

"Correct! And the superlative? Z is the—?"

" 'Worse' also?" asked Mr. Bloom hesitantly. It was evident he had never distinguished the fine difference in sound between the comparative and superlative forms of "bad."

"No, Mr. Bloom. It's not the *same* word, although it—er—sounds a good deal like it. Anyone? Come, come. It isn't hard. X is *bad*, Y is *worse*, and Z is the—?"

An embarrassed silence fell upon the class, which, apparently, had been using "worse" for both the comparative and superlative all along. Miss Mitnick blushed and played with her pencil. Mr. Bloom shrugged, conscious that he had given his all. Mr. Kaplan stared at the board, his mouth open, a desperate concentration in his eye.

"*Bad—worse*. What is the word you use when you mean 'most bad'?"

"Aha!" cried Mr. Kaplan suddenly. When Mr. Kaplan cried "Aha!" it signified that a great light had fallen on him. "I know! De exect void! So easy! *Ach!* I should know dat ven I vas wridink! *Bad—voise—*"

"Yes, Mr. Kaplan!" Mr. Parkhill was definitely excited.

"Rotten!"

Mr. Parkhill's eyes glazed once more, unmistakably. He shook his head dolorously, as if he had suffered a personal hurt. And as he wrote "W-O-R-S-T" on the blackboard there ran through his head, like a sad refrain, this latest manifestation of Mr. Kaplan's peculiar genius: "bad—worse—rotten; bad—worse…"

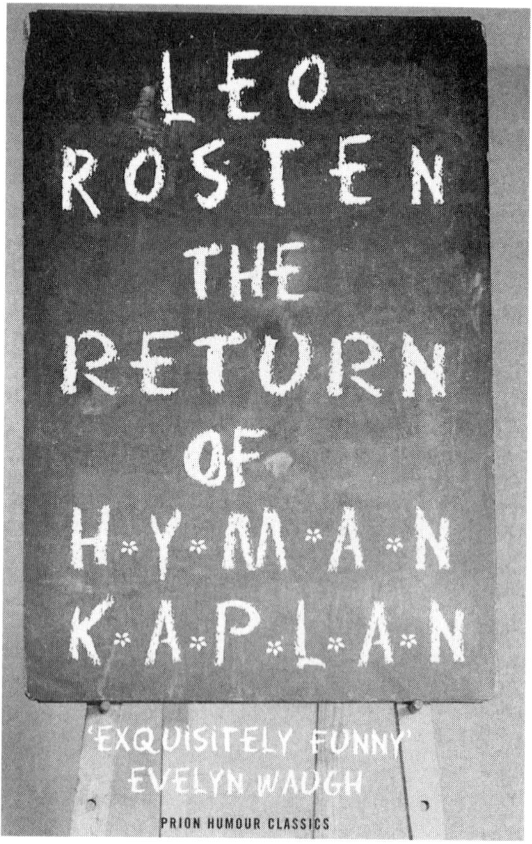
LEO
ROSTEN
THE
RETURN
OF
H*Y*M*A*N
K*A*P*L*A*N
'EXQUISITELY FUNNY'
EVELYN WAUGH
PRION HUMOUR CLASSICS

THE RETURN OF H*Y*M*A*N K*A*P*L*A*N

LEO ROSTEN

with a new introduction by HOWARD JACOBSON

"exquisitely funny"

Evelyn Waugh

Twenty years after his first collection of tales about that Don Quixote of adult education, Leo Rosten brought Hyman Kaplan back, by huge popular demand, for a second term in "Mr Pockheel's" class. Along with the other students who flunked the first time round – his old rival the conscientious Miss Mitnick, despairing Mrs Moskowitz and Sam Pinsky, Sancho Panza to Kaplan's Quixote – and some new faces, Olga Tarnova, the Slavic vamp and muttering Gus Matsoukas, a Greek among barbarians – Hyman Kaplan takes up where he left off, delighting in his performances upon the blackboard that provoke fierce classroom debates, cheerfully giving "spic" as the opposite of "span" and "delicatessen" as the plural of sandwiches, and confounding the poor Mr Parkhill with his own peculiar and unfathomable logic.

July 2000
1-85375-391-2
£8.99

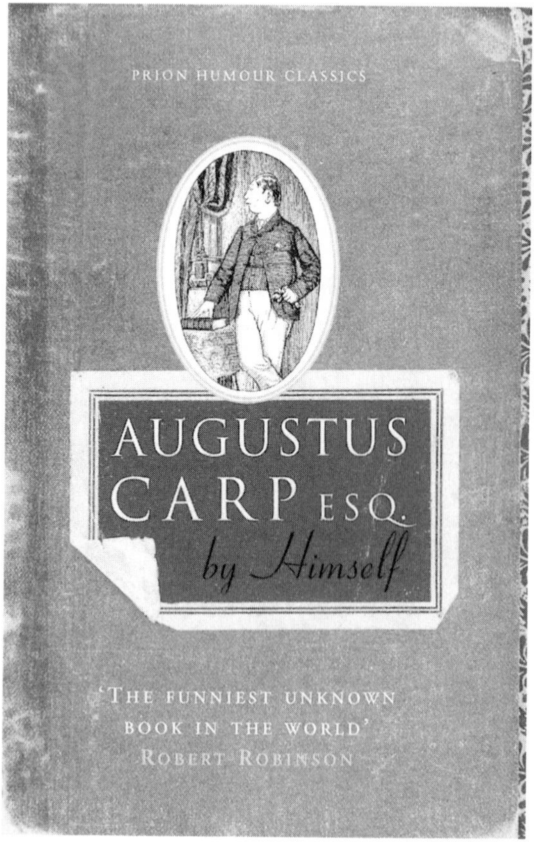
PRION HUMOUR CLASSICS
AUGUSTUS
CARP ESQ.
by Himself
'THE FUNNIEST UNKNOWN
BOOK IN THE WORLD'
ROBERT ROBINSON

Augustus Carp Esq

HENRY HOWARTH BASHFORD
with an introduction by Robert Robinson

"one of the great comic novels"
Anthony Burgess

First published in 1924, *Augustus Carp Esq* is a spoof autobiography: a deadpan comic account of a climb to the heights of mediocrity by a humorless, religious oaf, told in his own self-important, sermonising tone. A resident of Camberwell, London; Sunday-school superintendent and President of the St Potamus Purity League, Augustus is assiduous in exposing the sins and foibles of others while ignoring his own. Campaigning against lechery, drinking and smoking, he manages to indulge in plenty of other vices in the name of Christianity, justifying gluttony as a healthy appetite, informing on others as a devotion to the truth, and treating his mother as an unpaid skivvy in the name of patriarchal rectitude. The more seriously Carp takes himself the more ridiculous he becomes; his frequent falls from dignity and his absurd explanations are uproarious. With original illustrations by "Robin".

October 2000
1-85375-411-0
£8.99

"acid-tongued...peerless" Kirkus Review
MAPP & LUCIA
E F BENSON
PRION HUMOUR CLASSICS

Mapp and Lucia

E F BENSON

with a new introduction by Stephen Pile

"we will pay anything for Lucia books"

Noel Coward, Nancy Mitford, W H Auden

Mapp and Lucia is the prize jewel in E F Benson's series of Lucia novels tracing the enmity and fight for social supremacy between Miss Elizabeth Mapp and Emmeline Lucas (Lucia to her friends). In their acts of sabotage and jockeying for the position of cultural arbiter, Mapp and Lucia tear up the conventions of drawing-room diplomacy and enter a protracted conflict using fêtes, garden parties, musical soirées and bridge evenings as their deadly weapons, whilst Georgie, Lucia's companion and partner-in-pretension, as well as at the piano, and the other residents of the village of Tilling enjoy their most exciting social season yet. E F Benson's charming satirical bent turns the pretensions and snobberies of English village life into a deliciously vicious comedy.

June 2000
1-85375-390-4
£8.99

PRION HUMOUR CLASSICS
J L Carr
How
Steeple Sinderby Wanderers
Won the FA Cup

HOW STEEPLE SINDERBY WANDERERS WON THE FA CUP

J L CARR
with a new introduction by D J TAYLOR

"a wonderful book"
Observer

At the commission of Mr Fangfoss, chairman of the club, young Joe Gidner, failed theologian and greetings card poet, chronicles just how Steeple Sinderby (an unremarkable Fenland village, pop. 547) won Britain's premier sporting prize. This momentous journey from obscurity to national heroism is contrived by the serendipitous meeting of three great men: Fangfoss himself, Dr Kossuth, who invents six footballing postulations, and the Wanderers captain, Alex Slingsby. J L Carr's affectionate look at small-minded Middle England and the glories of God's own game, takes in love and death, bigamy, bigotry, old-fashioned English snobbery and, or course, blood and thunder football action.

December 1999
1-85375-363-7
£7.99

PRION HUMOUR CLASSICS
Diary of a
PROVINCIAL
LADY
E.M. Delafield
'Incredibly funny'
JILLY COOPER

The Diary of a Provincial Lady

E M DELAFIELD

with a new introduction by Jilly Cooper

"incredibly funny"

Jilly Cooper

Behind the rather prim and proper title lies the hilarious diary of a long-suffering and disaster-prone Devon lady of the 1930s and her forlorn attempts to keep her somewhat ramshackle household from falling into the chaos that continually beckons, while her reticent and undemonstrative husband Robert hides behind *The Times*. Beset on all sides by the havoc her children wreak, tricky servants, and merchants who gain the upper hand, she attempts to keep up her social standing within the community, particularly against the maddeningly patronising society dame Lady Boxe. A direct ancestor of *Bridget Jones' Diary*, this is a gently self-effacing, dry-witted tale of provincial social pretension and the inanities of daily domestic life. With original illustrations by Arthur Watt.

March 2000
1-85375-368-8
£7.99

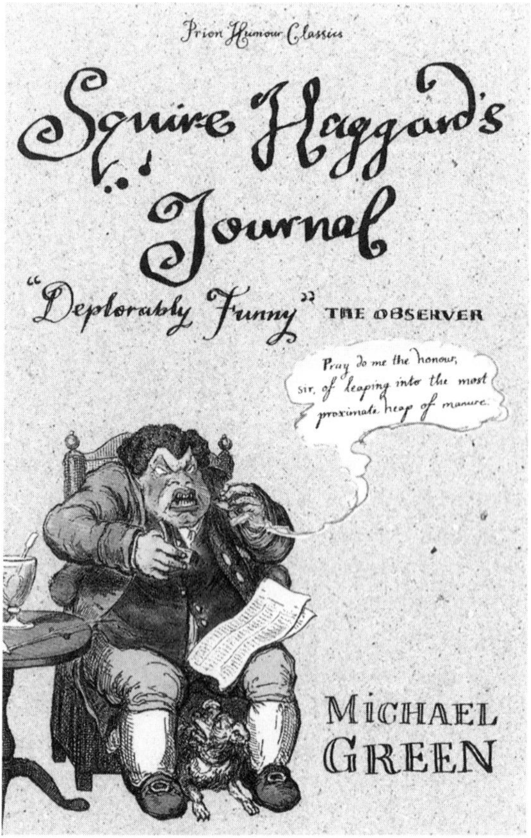
Prion Humour Classics
Squire Haggard's Journal
"Deplorably Funny" THE OBSERVER
Pray do me the honour, sir, of leaping into the most proximate heap of manure.
MICHAEL GREEN

Squire Haggard's Journal

MICHAEL GREEN

with a new introduction by the author

"deplorably funny"

Observer

Squire Haggard's Journal is a bawdy parody of a late-18th-century gentleman's diary. Amos Haggard is a Gargantuan, warty old toad of a character who, along with his idiotic son Roderick, spends most of his time carousing with prostitutes and servant girls, drinking copious amounts of Madeira wine, evicting the poor and firing his pistols at poachers, dissenters and foreigners. Eventually, in order to escape their unpaid debts and an impending duel, the lecherous and libidinous pair are forced to flee their estate and embark upon a grand tour, where they continue their vile debauched behaviour amid the crowned heads of Europe. Michael Green's comic classic – now reissued with a whole array of new episodes not included in the original – is a hilariously unreconstructed romp through the seamier side of 18th-century life that links Boswell to Blackadder.

October 2000
1-85375-399-8
£8.99

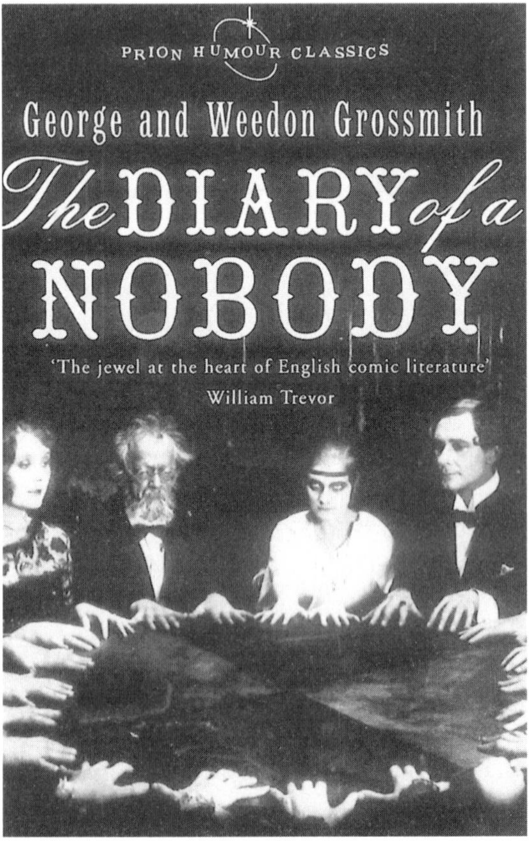
PRION HUMOUR CLASSICS
George and Weedon Grossmith
The DIARY of a NOBODY
'The jewel at the heart of English comic literature'
William Trevor

THE DIARY OF A NOBODY

GEORGE AND WEEDON GROSSMITH
with a new introduction by WILLIAM TREVOR

"a kind of Victorian Victor Meldrew"
Guardian

The eternally hard-done-by Charles Pooter is the most timeless comic character in English fiction – as alive and well today as he was when he first appeared in 1892. Abiding with his 'dear wife' Carrie in Holloway, London, Mr Pooter is a well-meaning city clerk and one of London's growing army of lower middle-class sub-urbanites set on improving their social standing. Aspiring to immortality, Mr Pooter embarks upon a diary in which he records all his mishaps and petty confrontations with tradesmen and neighbours, the trials of his wife's heedless indulgence in flights of fashion and the antics of his vagabond son Lupin, revealing himself as a lovable absurd Everyman: quietly self-satisfied, intent on keeping up appearances and ignorant of his own pretensions but quick to see those of others. His rose-tinted vision of his lot as one of dignified social grace is unwittingly exposed at every turn to hilarious effect. With illustrations by Weedon Grossmith.

December 1999
1-85375-364-5
£7.99

Three Men in a boat
'The funniest book I've ever read' VIC REEVES
Jerome K Jerome
prion humour classics

THREE MEN IN A BOAT

JEROME K JEROME
with a new introduction by Nigel Williams

"the only book I've fallen off a chair laughing at" *Vic Reeves*

Harris, George and J. are three Victorian idlers: amiable buffoons who love their food, their drink and their bachelor home comforts. They're none too keen on work either, especially George, who sleeps at a bank in the City from 10 till 4 each day "except Saturday when they put him outside at two". Yet their communal hypochondria has reached such a jittery level that they decide a change of scene from their usual lethargic routine is called for. And why not a trip up the Thames in an open boat to enjoy the natural simplicity of the river? As they set out armed with tobacco, whisky, a frying pan and a distinct lack of outdoor skills – accompanied by their faithful dog Montmorency, whose favourite pastime is attacking other canines – they discover that their idyll isn't quite all that they bargained for.

February 2000
1-85375-371-8
£7.99

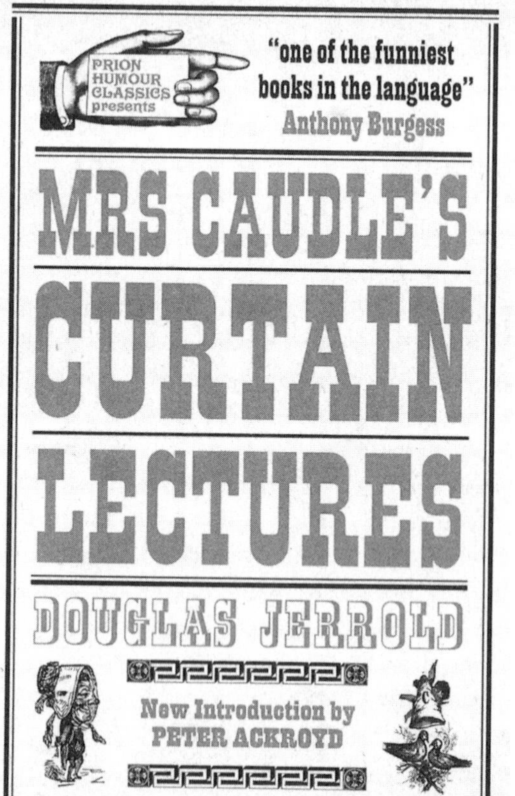
PRION
HUMOUR
CLASSICS
presents
"one of the funniest
books in the language"
Anthony Burgess
MRS CAUDLE'S
CURTAIN
LECTURES
DOUGLAS JERROLD
New Introduction by
PETER ACKROYD

Mrs Caudle's Curtain Lectures

DOUGLAS JERROLD
with a new introduction by PETER ACKROYD

"one of the funniest books in the language" *Anthony Burgess*

First published in *Punch* in 1845 and now reissued with the original illustrations by Charles Keene, Mrs Caudle's incessant bedtime petty lectures to her husband are just as hilarious and familiar today as they were then. Job Caudle is the original hen-pecked husband and Mrs Caudle the archetypal nag. Mr Caudle leads a quiet and well-intentioned life and looks forward to his few pleasures – usually a quiet drink with his friends. But in Mrs Caudle's eyes he can do no right, and night after night he is doomed to lie there, either feigning sleep or mustering the odd rejoinder, while Mrs Caudle nags, spins inconsistencies and turns molehills into mountains, construing his simplest acts – such as the loan of an umbrella – as monstrous deeds that will surely lead the whole family to death and damnation.

August 2000
1-85375-400-5
£8.99

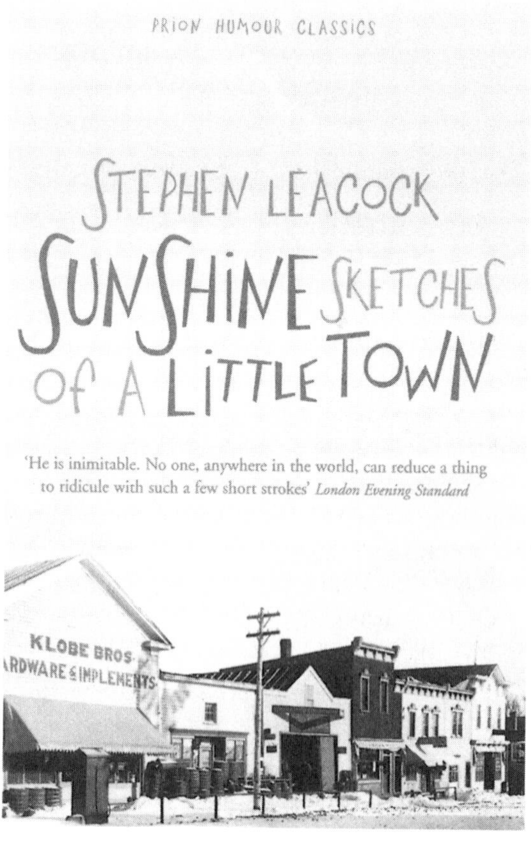
PRION HUMOUR CLASSICS
STEPHEN LEACOCK
SUNSHINE SKETCHES
OF A LITTLE TOWN
'He is inimitable. No one, anywhere in the world, can reduce a thing to ridicule with such a few short strokes' London Evening Standard
KLOBE BROS
ARDWARE & IMPLEMENTS

SUNSHINE SKETCHES OF A LITTLE TOWN

STEPHEN LEACOCK

with a new introduction by MORDECAI RICHLER

"There is no-one quite like Leacock, and no-one quite so good."

Tatler

Often described as Stephen Leacock's masterpiece, *Sunshine Sketches* is an amiable introduction to the North American hick town of Mariposa at the start of the 20th century – a satire of backwater life in which the inhabitants like to believe their world is the bustling, cosmopolitan apex of civilisation. In deftly drawn comic sketches with memorable characters, Leacock gently exposes the wily duplicity at work in the community, where the local church is up to its neck in an insurance scam, the Temperance club members carry hip flasks and farmers play off electioneering politicians to their own ends.

March 2000
1-85375-367-X
£8.99

ANITA LOOS
No Mother To Guide Her
INTRODUCTION BY KATHY LETTE

NO MOTHER TO GUIDE HER

ANITA LOOS
with a new introduction by KATHY LETTE

"intrepid satire"
Edmund Wilson

No Mother to Guide Her is Anita Loos' caustic comicbook tale of Hollywood in its 1920s heyday. Elmer Bliss, naive and implacably optimistic champion of the Southern Californian way, uses his newspaper column to defend the movie world's indiscretions from the scandal sheets. His crowning moment comes as he leaps to the protection of Miss Viola Lake, Hollywood's favourite clean-cut starlet, who is about to be accused of pill-popping and promiscuity during a murder trial that threatens to blow the lid off the film colony. With intimate ease Anita Loos sets up a fondly sardonic and devastatingly funny tour of the glorious artifice and excess that is Hollywood: dreadful architecture, tasteless fashion, bizarre religions, mass murder, sex, divorce, extravagant morals, industry nepotism and vacuous inhabitants wandering the boulevards in search of fame and fulfilment. With the original illustrations.

February 2000
1-85375-366-1
£7.99

SEVEN MEN AND TWO OTHERS

MAX BEERBOHM
with a new introduction by NIGEL WILLIAMS

"a masterpiece"
Clifton Fadiman

The tales that make up *Seven Men and Two Others* start out as a series of *faux* memoirs set amid London literary life in the precious *fin de siècle* era in which Beerbohm played such a leading role and stretch slowly into wonderfully absurd fantasy. With a sense of fun, a hint of nostalgia, razor-sharp satire and pitch-perfect parody, Beerbohm pulls at the affected nature of the whole literary scene – lamentable authors, wily agents and ridiculous weekend salons at country seats. Each tale is based around an individual from Enoch Soames, the execrable poet who makes a pact with the devil, to the literary feuders 'Hilary Maltby and Stephen Braxton' in these hilarious tales which have been classed by Lord David Cecil as "the finest expression of the comic spirit produced by any English writer."

February 2001
1-85375-415-3
£8.99